Glimpses

of

An Abundant Life

Frank W. Donaldson

Glimpses of An Abundant Life

© 2011

by Frank W. Donaldson

Printed in the United States of America

ISBN 978-1460981184

Acknowledgements

I am very grateful to my good friend of 65 years, Wendell Givens, for his advice, suggestions, and the proofreading of many of my stories. I was shocked and broken-hearted to learn that on Saturday, December 9, 2006, he passed away. A truly fine man. I regret that I did not finish my book in his lifetime.

My thanks also are given to my daughter, Susan Irvin, and Cumberland Law School secretary, Judy McAlister, for much typing-done pleasantly and with a lovely smile.

Lastly, to my son-in-law, Richie Irvin, for the final touches.

To Patti,

A Most Precious Love

~ *Contents* ~

FOREWORD

Some people look forward to enjoying the peace and tranquility of retirement, sitting under their own fig tree. I have no fig tree and don't want one. Please don't misunderstand; I don't belittle the comfortable retirement. But for me, now, there's still work to be done. I have memories to share.

Several years ago my wife Patti and I stood just inside the main entrance to Jarnigan Cemetery in Morristown, Tennessee, and pondered the life of the Revolutionary War participant whose statue stood tall before us. The acclaimed old soldier, my great–great grandfather, was in full military uniform. Word has been passed down for generations that William Donaldson had been mustered out of General George Washington's army in New Jersey in November 1783 and had walked 700 miles to his farm in east Tennessee.

William was born more than 250 years ago. He was past 40 when he made the postwar two-month trek home.

Ten years later my great-great granddad moved his family into a log home he had built in what is now Russellville, next door to Morristown. That home, where my grandfather and my father were born, still stands and is occupied.

In 1992, the year before its 200th anniversary, Patti and I visited the old home and the people then living there. But how little we knew of William Donaldson, the dwelling's first occupant. As we stood before his statue (since removed) at Jarnigan we wondered:

What was this Revolutionary War participant really like? For example, did he smoke or chew tobacco? Did he perhaps make moonshine whiskey or blackberry wine?

Was he involved in politics?

Did he curse and have a temper, or was he quiet, cool, and reserved?

We had learned that he owned slaves, as did many people back then, but how many?

Some ten years before the Civil War began, his grandson, also William, had freed his slaves, some of whom he had inherited from his father.

Did the war veteran treat his wife with respect?

What was William Donaldson's religion? Was he Presbyterian, as were many Donaldsons who came to America from Scotland?

Could he read and write?

The questions-without-answers were endless because my great-great forebearer apparently left no diary or other written record—no letters, no nothing—that would suggest what kind of person he was.

That day as Patti and I stood admiring the statue and in thoughts through the years since then, I resolved not to leave my children, their children and others to come with no clues about my life, my experiences, my family, and my observations.

Thus in this modest volume for family, for friends and interested others, in my 89th year I share my memories, my yesterdays, glimpses of an abundant life.

William Donaldson Monument,
Jarnigan Cemetery, Morristown, Tennessee

Note to the Foreword

The stories that follow in this mostly anecdotal autobiography were written over a period of years. As the reader will observe, there are a few times a story may relate to another one, but no story relies upon another, though there are instances when a dab of repetition promotes clarity.

ANCESTRY

Those who came before me were hearty souls.

TWO MEN OF VALOR

My great-great grandfather, William Donaldson, according to the family legend, was mustered out of military service in New Jersey at the end of the Revolutionary War in November 1783. (I referred to this old soldier in the foreword to this book.) He was 45 years of age and walked home to east Tennessee, about 700 miles.

Of course, leaving New Jersey in November meant that a great deal of his hike was during winter, especially difficult when he crossed the Smokies. Winters back then are said to have been even colder than they are today.

The old Revolutionary War veteran may have arrived home financially strapped. I say this because he and his family did not move into the house he built in Russellville until 1793, approximately 10 years after his return. He resided there for 26 years, dying in 1819, shortly before his 81st birthday.

Great-great Grandfather was an excellent craftsman. (That doesn't run in the family, not with me anyway.) The house he erected not only still stands but is occupied and in good condition.

Following my wonderful Kingsport, Tennessee, relative, Mrs. Paul (Dotty) Royston's directions, Patti and I easily located the house and visited there on the eve of the 200th anniversary of its first occupancy. The owner showed us about the place and described some details of its construction. Our host also said that he planned to have the place entered in the appropriate historical register. I hope that he did.

The two-story house has two unusually wide chimneys, one on each side, and large logs chinked with clay comprise its walls.

At one time many poplar, pine, and maple trees grew on the premises. The logs in the house appeared to me to be poplar. The building sits on a knoll.

Donaldson Home - Russellville, Tennessee built in 1793

On April 13, 1823, my paternal grandfather, William Jordan Donaldson, entered the world in that house. Papa, John Worley Donaldson, was born in the house on February 5, 1852. So were Papa's six brothers and four sisters.

During the Civil War, Yankee General Humphries lived in the place several weeks. My Grandmother Amanda is reported to have lived there at that time with three children. But my Grandfather William Jordan Donaldson, grandson of the Revolutionary War soldier, was not there. He was in Kentucky during a portion of the war. Papa told me when I was a boy that Kentucky was sufficiently neutral for his dad to be able to avoid the Confederate military draft.

Nonetheless, a daughter was born to Amanda in 1864.

Grandfather William had freed his slaves several years before the Civil War, saying he wanted no more of slavery.

As far as I have learned, grandfather is the only draft-dodger in the family tree — and under the circumstances I'm proud of him for not defending slavery.

The gutsy old Revolutionary War guy was buried in the Jarnigan cemetery at Morristown, several miles west of Russellville. Near the Jarnigan entrance is an attractive monument for great-great grandfather William, with this inscription in large letters near the base:

DONALDSON

REVOLUTIONARY SOLDIER

In the Bethesda Cemetery, not far from his homeplace, is a small foot marker for the other gutsy guy, William, the one who had freed his slaves, the one who had come to believe that slavery was unjust.

CHILD OF *GRAND* PARENTS

John Worley Donaldson

When I was born, Papa was 69 and Mama 40. In my young adulthood I sometimes wondered if their advanced ages at my birth would somehow result in my having a short lifespan. That did not occur.

Typically and by nature, children born to young parents may reasonably expect to have longer life spans than their parents. On the other hand, as in my case, when parents are older — especially if one is past normal retirement age when a child is born — the question arises: Will the child be healthy and can it expect longevity?

As I write, my age is three years beyond Papa's at his death (86) and 13 years more than Mama's at her

Frank Donaldson

Eight and a half months old
Morristown, Tennessee -
1922

passing. My health has been good, better than Mama's, not quite up to Papa's.

When I avoided the flu bug (or it bypassed me) during the winter, I seldom lost a teaching day at the law school. Also, my mental processes remain strong at 89. During the past several years I could have taught full-time at the Cumberland Law School, rather than part-time, if I so chose. The dean asked me twice to consider teaching additional courses, i.e., again teaching full-time, even offering me a choice of subjects. So that I might pursue other interests I declined his offers.

Fortunately, Mama and Papa also continued mentally sharp through their senior years.

If Papa had been living, he would have reminded us that on February 5, 2002, he would have been 150. On July 12, 2001, Mama's cake would have been covered with 120 candles.

I'm grateful that the elderly gentleman and his mature bride chose to do as they did.

Mildred (Andrew's wife), Frank, Andrew,
Jane (David's wife), Bernice, and David Donaldson
Late Summer - 1990

John Worley Donaldson with Bernice, Andrew, and Frank
Phenix City, Alabama - 1925

*John Worley Donaldson and wife, Susie Appleby Donaldson, with
children Frank Worley and Bernice Cornelia Donaldson
Morristown, Tennessee - 1923*

*John Worley Donaldson
with Frank (left) and Bernice
Phenix City, Alabama - 1924*

*Andrew (left) and Frank Donaldson
Phenix City - 1920's*

GROWING UP IN SIN CITY

In the 1930's Mama always got upset reading what she called "false reports" of Sin City gambling and other vices. And why shouldn't she have been upset? Our Phenix City family lived in a different world from the evildoers she read about.

DEEP ROOTS

Papa regretted moving to Alabama. Most of that regret was leaving east Tennessee. Especially in his 80s, he longed to return to his roots where he had spent his first seven decades.

In the 19th century Papa had taken a wife in Morristown; they reared three sons and a daughter. He also had become a widower there, burying his wife of 40-plus years in Morristown's Emma Jarnigan Cemetery.

Mentioning Papa's yearning to return to his former "home" is not saying he moped about it, but it came through. Even today I think how unfortunate for him in his last years to live in one place and wish he were in another.

For two-score years, Papa and his brother George owned and operated Donaldson Brothers, a wholesale grocery business. Soon after he and Mama married in 1920, Papa sold his share to George.

Then in 1924 (I was 3 in September), John Worley Donaldson, 72, and his bride, my mama, Susie Appleby Donaldson, 43, left Papa's homeplace and moved to Phenix City, Alabama, later known as Sin City. Mama owned 40 acres just inside the western city limits. Mama had inherited the property from her father, thus she had returned to her roots. My parents had pooled their resources, his cash and her unimproved land. Their venture was successful for them and then for Mama during the 19 years she was a widow.

For me the whole deal was a bonanza. I don't mean money wise; I refer to location. I grew up where I could hunt, fish, and romp in the fields, woods, and pastures. And I enjoyed a summertime "swimming hole" in Holland Creek close to home— a real country life.

David T. Donaldson
Age 15

The schools were nearby as were our neighbors, so there were plenty of playmates.

Downtown Phenix City and Columbus, Georgia, were within easy walking distance. Therefore we seldom rode the

Columbus City bus that made a stop only a few blocks from our house.

In addition to building our homeplace, Papa built 10 rental houses and bought three more. This assured Mama an income for her life.

When Papa passed away, Mama had the responsibility to complete the rearing of their four offspring: me, Bernice (Nena), Andrew (Stokely), and David, born in that order. Mama had sufficient income for us to live on, even during the remaining Depression years, as she carefully guarded every penny.

Andrew Stokely Donaldson 1939

Papa had been even more frugal. I thought as a boy, and still do, that he was miserly. His Scottish forebearers would have been proud. Papa was 29 years older than Mama, so I'm sure that he was anticipating the time his widow would have sole financial obligation for her family.

During the 1930s the cotton mills, big employers of the workers of Phenix City and Columbus, were shut down, or practically so,

Bernice Cornelia Donaldson 1939

making rent money, Mama's income, hard to come by. Although some tenants could not pay, or fully pay when rent was due, I don't recall my parents ever evicting anyone.

My years in Phenix City (1924-39) were centered at 1604 21st Street, a white frame house. A few feet from our back door a well provided our water. It wasn't running water because we had no pump.

At the back of the house, behind the garage where Papa protected his Model-T, was the privy (the outhouse). Underneath the privy was what we today might call a septic tank, although there were no field lines. The daily paper and frequently a Sears and Roebuck catalog served dual purposes.

Most streets in Phenix City were dirt, i.e., "unpaved," as was the one in front of our house, and for several blocks between our place and downtown. We kids walked such streets (no sidewalks) to both Summerville Grade School and Central High.

Donaldson Foursome
Bernice Cornelia, David Turner,
Frank Worley, Andrew Stokely
Phenix City, Alabama - 1929

In "Sin City" the streets downtown, near the Chattahoochee River and the gambling joints, were paved, of course.

In the 1920s and 1930s, my growing-up years in Sin City, gambling and various nefarious activities there were rampant, but it all occurred in a world unknown to me, my family, and our neighbors. We could just as well have been living on a different planet. We never had to lock our doors at home, never had anything stolen, and in all my years there as a happy kid never remember seeing a policeman or any other law enforcement officer in our neighborhood.

Children walked safely to school, and we teenage boys went fearlessly wherever we chose, day or night. We could not have led a more peaceful life; tranquility reigned.

The widespread media-reported mischief just didn't exist in our world. Nonetheless, Papa yearned to return to the rolling hills of east Tennessee, the blue grass area he truly loved.

He made a few visits back; then in November 1938, at age 86, he was buried in Emma Jarnigan Cemetery in Morristown.

Papa didn't pass to me his Scotsman's blood of frugality. However, I will confess that somehow, someway, I had at one time in my bloodstream a very close feel for the east Tennessee countryside where Papa was born and lived so many years.

Don't misunderstand, I don't desire, much less yearn, to live in Hamblen County, Tennessee, again as did my father. But here I will reveal a little secret.

More than three decades ago I was Cumberland Law School's professor representative at a conference conducted by the University of Tennessee School of Law in Knoxville. While there I pondered this thought: Were I offered a teaching position with the U.T. law school would I seriously consider it? Remarkable, at the time U.T. was the only other law school in the United States for which I felt a little tug.

You see, the university is only 40 or so miles from my Morristown birthplace, so perhaps it was a "home" tug of sorts.

Well, U.T. never made me an offer and I can happily report I'm glad, because I might have been tempted to accept it.

Looking back 35 years I like to think that family members in Alabama, other nearby relatives, Birmingham area friends, and my attachment to the Cumberland School of Law would have overridden any fleeting desire I had to get near my east Tennessee roots. My deepest roots are really in Alabama and always have been.

A TURKEY AND VEGGIES

In today's society one is not likely to see an 11 or 12-year-old boy pulling a little red wagon along an unpaved street, especially if he is hawking butterbeans and black-eyed peas.

In the early 1930s many of my neighbors in the western part of Phenix City, Alabama, saw me doing just that in late spring and early summer. I was going door to door asking "the lady of the house" to have a look at my fresh, garden-grown beans and peas.

I had helped plant the seeds, hoe grass from around the growing plants, quashed many beetles on the leaves of the bean vines, and helped pick the beans and peas. Even so, I was a minor player in the family's gardening, but I was the sole salesperson, pulling my little wagon, walking the dirt streets of our severely economically depressed city.

Unshelled butterbeans sold for 25 cents a basket (no tax), probably close to a peck. A quarter wasn't much payment for the sweat and time my family had invested in the garden, but 25 cents would purchase five loaves of sliced bread.

I have no recollection of what I was paid for black-eyed peas, but they didn't fetch as much as a quarter per sale as did the butterbeans.

Admission to a movie was a dime and a bag of popcorn cost a nickel, so for a while that summer I could finance Saturday afternoons. Just where the rest of my earnings went I'm not sure, but I am sure I had to make an accounting with Mama, so that some of the money found its way to the grocery store.

Times then were truly tough. During the worst of the Depression, our school teachers either were paid in script or not paid at all. There was little or no money for schools to buy supplies— sometimes even none for chalk. So periodically efforts were made to raise money for schools. That's when I got back into selling, although only for a little while.

One November, perhaps the one following my busy year in the garden and selling veggies, the school provided my neighbors an opportunity to have a turkey for Thanksgiving. All they had to do was spend a little money for a chance to win one in a school fundraiser.

I sold tickets door-to-door at 10 cents each. The gobbler was to be raffled a few days before the holiday.

Other kids were recruited and made "sales". Each of us made a big push to sell the most chances, to collect the most dimes.

How many chances did I sell? I dunno, but it was a bunch.

At the raffle the tickets were collected from all us grade school salesmen and placed in a basket. A teacher was asked to draw the winning ticket and announce the number printed on it. The person holding the winning ticket number excitedly responded, raising his hand as he moved to the front of the room to collect his gobbler.

Would you believe I was the winner? That's right! The kid who had sold the most tickets also won the turkey. I had invested one dime for a ticket and walked away the winner. Looking back, I'm glad I was among friends.

Mama cooked the bird and we had a big Thanksgiving Day feast. That surely was the only day during my youth that I provided all the meat for a meal.

Although Mama usually kept her thoughts to herself, I expect she pondered in her heart whether she did right letting her son sell chances, even buying one for himself. Mama probably prayed that her son would not become a gambler. After all, don't forget that the Donaldsons, as noted earlier, lived in Phenix City, widely publicized at the time as Sin City because of its underworld activities, mainly gambling.

Our home was across town from the gambler's dens and Mama knew those several blocks would be an easy walk for her young son. But she really didn't need to be anxious because that was a journey I never made.

TAKE CARE OF PAPA

In the winter after I turned 12 years old in September, in the dark of our barnyard, Papa fell over a sleeping cow and injured his ribs. At age 81 his recovery was slow.

I felt some responsibility to both Papa and Mama for not preventing the accident.

One evening well after dark Papa remembered that he needed to return to the barnyard for a reason I don't recall. Perhaps it was to let a cow out of a stall, or to check one of the barnyard gates to be sure it was securely fastened. Whatever, when Papa started to leave the house, Mama said, "Go with your Papa."

At age 12 I knew Mama's concern, for Papa's eyesight was failing. I think nighttime increased the vision problem. Without being specific, Mama had sent me a clear message: "Take care of your father."

The evening was pitch black. I remember that I could not see my hand in front of my face, even though my eyesight was unusually strong.

Papa and I had just entered the barnyard through a small gate when Papa tripped over a cow lying between the gate and the barn. Papa was a strong man and not given to complaining, but now he was hurt and in agony.

Slowly we made our way back to the house, and as one might expect of a 12-year-old, I ran to Mama and blurted, "Papa's hurt."

Mama took over and helped make Papa as comfortable as she could. Two others also were hurt, Mama doubly so because Papa was hurt, and because her son had not done the very job his Mama had asked as he accompanied his Papa to the barn. I was emotionally hurt. I felt I had let both parents down. If someone was to trip over a cow it should have been me; then Papa wouldn't have gotten hurt. That's the way my 12-year-old mind worked.

Mama could have lectured, even chastised me for not being alert, but she uttered no word of criticism. Her attention was on Papa.

Even after Papa recovered from the cracked ribs, Mama never mentioned my inattention. However, it was not long before I had substantially more duties at the barn — without Papa.

SANDY STREETS AND SUNDAY SCHOOL

On February 1, 1934, I made a public profession of faith in Jesus Christ as my Lord and Savior and was baptized in the Pilgrim Congregational Church in Phenix City. I was 12.

Mama and Papa had sent me to Sunday School from the time I was little more than a toddler. Perhaps I exaggerate, but I was really a little guy and my parents didn't take me. They sent me. I marched off, well before starting first grade at Summerville School.

We lived at 1604 21st Street, so I walked unpaved streets seven or eight blocks to what was then United Congregational Church. But the United church lost the "united" when a schism developed among members.

After the split I attended Sunday School with the people who had pulled away. We met in a neighbor's house a block from where I lived — a real convenience for a 6 or 7-year-old boy.

A year later I began walking the sandy streets seven or eight blocks from our house to the new "Pilgrim"

Frank in first grade, Summerville Grade School - 1928

Congregational Church building (now First Congregational). Autos were sparse and hence of no real concern. I had to cross the Central of Georgia Railroad tracks, which didn't bother me or my parents.

The new church building was brick veneer. It had a sanctuary and two or three Sunday school rooms. In front and on the sides of the building was a good deal of open land. The railroad tracks were a block or two north. Several houses were nearby behind the church.

On Sundays, before Sunday school, there was a general assembly in Pilgrim's auditorium. Mr. Jackson was Sunday

School Superintendent and Mrs. Rowland was my teacher. Their names are the only ones I recall. I don't even remember the pastor's name. That suggests either that I was not at worship service very often or that the pastor was unimpressive.

I confess that attending regular preaching (worship) service was not on my agenda and my parents did not insist that it be. Regular attendance would come in my college years.

Papa was a Presbyterian, but he did not attend church. Mama was a Methodist and she went to First Methodist in Phenix City only once in a while. After Papa died, Mama attended church regularly until just before her death in 1957.

I became a Congregationalist because that church was near my home. My membership became official upon my profession of Jesus as my Savior and being baptized (sprinkled) at Pilgrim. At that time I was given a small New Testament that I still have 70 plus years later.

Carlton Shavor, who lived about a block from the church, became one of my real close teenage buddies, a friendship that developed mostly through Sunday school. Carlton learned to play the piano by practicing at church and while still a teenager became church pianist.

For two weeks in June we kids had Vacation Bible School with punch and cookies for refreshments. Most of my memories there are from Depression years. Phenix City was a cotton mill town, so I'm sure someone sacrificed so we could have those refreshments. The mills usually were idle during the 1930s, functioning for short work weeks, if at all.

During the hard times of the 1930s there were many very poor people in Phenix City. A number of those attended Pilgrim and I'm sure some of them occasionally worshiped on empty stomachs. Times have changed and the people there today are not hungry, although some may need spiritual food. But, isn't that likely anywhere, even if a church is nearby?

If the Pilgrim Congregational Church had not been built prior to the Depression, it probably wouldn't have been built at all: too few members, too much cost.

The little church building still stands. Sunday morning worship is at 11 o'clock.

MY ROLE MODEL

First cousin Forrest Shavers, son of my mother's sister, Cornelia (Aunt Nena), was my role model in Phenix City. I never had another.

Forrest was seven years my senior. There were times when he tutored me without my knowing he was doing so. Other times he made it plain that tutoring was taking place.

I couldn't have fared better. He

Forrest Shavers as a young teenager in Phenix City, Alabama about 1930

neither smoked nor drank. Why he didn't smoke I don't know, but it probably was the expense. For all the years I was his "little brother", money (20 cents) for a pack of cigarettes was hard to come by.

Why Forrest never drank alcoholic beverages was clear, and I never forgot. Even if he had had monetary riches, no alcoholic drink would ever have touched his lips. His father was an alcoholic, in those days known as a drunkard. He died when Forrest was a small child, but not so small that Forrest did not have imbedded in his memory the gut-wrenching times Mr. Shavers' drinking was a problem.

Forrest became so upset that he never wanted to be near an intoxicant. And he didn't get near one or allow one to be near him.

We never had to discuss the problem; it was a given that to him whiskey and beer were evil in light of what they had done to his father.

I'm sure, too, that Forrest could have quoted scripture to support his opposition to drink. I say that because he once quoted a New Testament verse to me, although on a different subject, that so grabbed my attention I have remembered it for 70 years. On an occasion (I can't recall full details) I pointed to a man and exclaimed, "Look at that fool," whereupon Forrest admonished me, "Do you not know the Bible says to call a person a fool will get you hell fire and damnation?"

Not a precise quote, but close. After looking it up, Matthew 5:22, KJV, I decided never again to say to a person "you fool". Nonetheless I'm sure that since that teaching, many times I've skirted Jesus' words by remarking that a person's comments or actions were foolish, but never that the individual was a fool.

Another lesson, clearly intended as such, occurred when I was 12 or 13. Forrest gave me my first and only driving lesson. I never actually drove the vehicle, but I sat behind the steering wheel. The lesson could have been given on a chalkboard and perhaps been as effective; instead we sat in a car parked in front of Forrest's home and practiced shifting gears.

The old stick-shift auto had four gears, referred to by my instructor as low, second, drive and reverse. He explained the gear positions and how each functioned while I moved the gear stick from one position to another while moving my left foot to push in the clutch with each shift, trying hard not to make a clashing noise while shifting.

The street in front of Aunt Nena's house was unpaved, level and bore little traffic, but there was no way Forrest would let me drive, even a few blocks. He would take no chances with this kid behind the steering wheel of his boss's vehicle.

Eight or nine years later I got my next driving lesson. I gave it to myself. That took place when I purchased a 1937 Chevy business coupe and "jerked" it away from the dealer's lot, making plain to anyone watching that the 21-year-old second lieutenant was not ready for a speedway, not even ready for downtown traffic. Somehow I managed to get back to the airbase in time to give a cadet his flight lesson. Maybe that was because I knew how the gears functioned.

Forrest loved baseball, and it was fun for me to grow up loving the game (I still do) and watching Forrest play.

In those days there were many local ball teams, often referred to as "semi-pro" because the players got a few perks.

Forrest was not a pitcher but he liked to try pitching and he knew a good bit about it, so he set aside time to teach me. He showed me, a right-hander, how to hold the ball just before releasing it for various pitches, how to throw a curve, what he called a "drop," a fastball and an "in" on which the ball breaks in toward a right-handed batter. We practiced with Forrest as the catcher.

My pitching in sandlot ball showed that I never practiced enough — not nearly enough. Let's just say that opposing batters had a happy time when I was on the mound. Had Forrest seen those games, he would have been chagrined that his pupil was serving up unintended batting practice.

When my teacher/cousin was in high school, he had a newspaper route in across-the-river Columbus, Georgia. "Throwing" the Columbus Enquirer meant getting up before dawn and biking from home to Broad Street. On occasion I helped him fold the papers, not roll them as they arrive at our home today.

For home delivery the Enquirer was folded so that it could be tossed flat onto a driveway, walkway or porch. If the front door was not flush with the floor the paper might slide into the living room!

By assisting with the paper route, I got real insight into the character of my role model. He was an early riser, never absent, never late. I've always been an early riser; did I get the habit from my role model? Perhaps, but I remember that as a little kid I got up early on cold mornings to build a fire in our fireplace.

Newspaper subscribers paid weekly; Saturday morning was collection time. Subscription was only 25 cents a week, but some subscribers had to be dunned. Forrest made clear to them that they wouldn't get a paper if they were more than two weeks behind. He was equally gracious to those who paid on time and those who didn't.

In all our years together I never heard Forrest use profanity, even with tightwads. He spoke softly, pleasantly all his life. In his late 70s he walked slowly up stadium steps at St. Petersburg's Lange Field for our annual visit to baseball's spring training. We enjoyed major-league baseball only a few blocks from Forrest's home. His gracious manner had not changed from the days when he was a paperboy and later ballplayer.

When my friend/role model reached 25, he and Jewell Kirkland (and indeed she is a jewel) married — and they stayed married 53 years, until his death in 1993.

Once in my freshman year at Southern Union Junior College, Jewell drove me the 75 miles to campus. En route we shopped at a dime store in Opelika and a salesgirl asked if we were on our honeymoon. Jewell replied that we were not, but at age seventeen I relished the compliment.

During a World War II furlough I visited Forrest and Jewell, and they lent me their car to ride around Phenix City and to visit Fort Benning. Apparently Forrest had known all along I would be a better driver than baseball pitcher.

THE HUNTERS

The terrible Depression of the 1930s took its toll on millions of Americans, black and white. I was fortunate; I never went hungry and had shoes and warm clothes during those Depression winters. But that was not the case for some youngsters my age in Phenix City.

Of course, I didn't know at the time that the bad economic conditions caused great anxiety for parents. Many must have wondered where their next meal was coming from.

Some families, a lot of them I expect, depended upon their unemployed breadwinner to shoot birds and wild game to put meat on the table. My family did not depend on my hunting ability for meat, although I hunted a lot strictly for fun. In the Depression years I never saw a deer, or a turkey, or even an armadillo, because in our area in southeast Alabama there were none to see.

So, hungry hunters sought rabbits, squirrels, doves and quail, even opossums. These satisfied many a hungry palate and empty stomach. But the supply was limited. There was even a limit to a breadwinner's ability to buy shotgun shells for hunting. This was brought home to me in a dramatic way in about 1935 or 1936 in a large field of broom sage several hundred yards behind my Aunt Cornelia's house (Aunt Nena, we called her) in Phenix City.

I was hunting there, on the western edge of town, looking for either birds or rabbits when a black man, age 35 to 45, and I met in the field. The sage was tall and we were fairly close before we saw each other. In each hand he held a rock the size of a baseball. "Whatcha got?" I asked. "Looking for a rabbit," he replied. "My kids need some meat."

He could see I hadn't shot anything. I said, "Haven't even seen a bird, except maybe a field lark," which was not worth shooting it was so small.

I held a 12-gauge double-barreled Lefever shotgun that had belonged to my dad and which I had standing permission to use. "Be careful, Son," my parents had instructed me. In earlier years they had given me essential safety pointers.

"How you gonna get a rabbit with a rock?" I inquired.

Answering my question, the man said, "I look for a rabbit that is bedded down; it's easier to hit."

I knew that "bedded down" meant a rabbit was nestled in a curled bundle under a sage. A rabbit's instinct tells it to lie still so it won't be spotted. The camouflage is almost perfect for a rabbit lying still in December broom sage.

The man moved on, looking closely at the base of each sage hoping to spot meat for supper.

Later I surmised that perhaps he had a gun at home but no money to buy shells. Or perhaps he had pawned his gun for cash to buy food. Times were unbelievably tough.

The economy was so tight, jobs and money so scarce that several hoboes in Phenix City and across the river Columbus, Georgia, periodically travelled on a train to Opelika. They carried empty burlap sacks, and in Opelika they would catch a freight train headed back to Phenix City and Columbus. While on the train they would climb atop a coal car, fill their sacks with lump coal and when the train got inside the city limits of Phenix City (where the tracks ran alongside our cow pasture), they would heave off the sacks of coal.

When the train slowed, the men would hop off, walk back along the tracks to "their" coal sacks and lug them home. Not once did I see or hear of a railroad detective or other police detaining any of these men.

Had I chosen to do so, I could have carried off a bunch of coal sacks, but I never touched them. We had coal delivered to our house.

I left my fellow hunter in the sage as he moved slowly through the field. Absent a miracle, he probably sought meat in vain. I hope the miracle he needed occurred.

On that day I never saw a rabbit or even a partridge or a dove. But no matter in my case, I knew we would have food on the supper table. I also knew that coal was burning in our fireplace.

No, we were not well off money-wise, just exceptionally fortunate to have ample food, clothing and shelter.

MAMA'S FLOWERS

In our yard in Phenix City, Mama had a fenced area set aside for her own flower garden. She strove to have flowers blooming all year. She also wanted her eldest son to work with her among the flowers.

That part of her striving was mostly in vain because I was seldom disposed to be helpful. I just wasn't very cooperative; there were too many weeds and too much unwanted grass, and it all grew too fast. All of which meant that fooling with Mama's flowers required a lot of time I'd rather have spent with my buddies, or engaged in another self-centered activity like building model airplanes.

Besides, we had a huge vegetable garden, fruit trees, chickens, cows, at times a hog, fences to mend, and caged pigeons (mine), all of which required a variety of chores, day-in and day-out.

So, Mama's flower garden was put on the back burner. There were times the vegetable garden was prettier; at least it had fewer weeds.

After I left home for college, Mama sold the home place, leaving her special flower spot for someone else to tend, or to make excuses for not doing so.

At her new home in Birmingham, Mama had no garden of any kind, but she was blessed with one of the most beautiful flowering trees that graced any yard. Each spring as I looked upon her gorgeous flowering crabapple tree, I saw more blossoms than Mama ever had in her special garden in Phenix City.

Although the crabapple blossoms were magnificent for only a couple of weeks, the sight of the blossoms still lingers in my memory.

I'm sure Mama envisioned those blossoms all year. The branches of that special gift from God almost touched her bedroom windows, giving her a chance to enjoy the blossoms' sweet, sweet aroma, and even in April after the flower petals had fallen to the ground, she enjoyed their beauty.

I know this was so, for as I write this on a cool, cloudy December day, in my mind's eye I see Mama's tree in full bloom.

The thought strikes me: If I could relive those childhood days, would I act differently and assist Mama in her special garden? Surely I could tend a couple of rosebushes all summer; perhaps plant a few bulbs in December. But would I? Probably not without a lot of prodding. After all, boys will be boys and I just couldn't be there when needed. Chances are, another chore or personal preference would take priority, or playmates would pass our yard beckoning with their bats and gloves.

"Those boys are a nuisance," Mama would say when I yielded to their call. She was so right. But I'm glad that neither

they nor I nor anyone ever hindered her enjoyment of the
flowering crabapple.

THE WRESTLERS

A 15-year-old black boy and I sat in the woods about
halfway between our Phenix City homes and chatted for a long
time before we wrestled. We were the same age and size and
enrolled in public schools, segregated, of course. Although we
lived less than half a mile apart, we were on separate planets.

We sat alone in the world. No one could see us sitting
among the trees and later wrestling. We probably began wrestling
because we ran out of conversation. Or perhaps we just wanted to
test each other's physical prowess. Whatever brought on the
wrestling, I got the better of him. But there was a downside. Later
on, something about that day disturbed me. Still does.

I well recall that when we began our tussle, I noted the
youngster was very strong, stronger than I was. However, as we
competed, I noticed that he seemed to wear down faster than I did
and I wondered why.

Much later it dawned on me. The year was 1936 and the
United States was in the middle of an economic depression.
Multitudes of people were hungry and malnourished. Some kids
in my school went barefoot all winter.

Years later I would learn that, at the time my buddy and I
were wrestling, a lovely 8-year-old child living with her mom and

dad 150 miles away in Helena, Alabama, was wearing a dress made from a flour-sack. Thirteen years later, while wearing a borrowed wedding dress, she would become my wife.

So, it has occurred to me as I look back to that wrestling match, my opponent may have been at a substantial disadvantage. We ate well at my house, always. We had a large, productive garden; one, sometimes two milk cows, chickens, an abundance of eggs, and in the winter there were vegetables that had been canned fresh from our garden.

In the community of shotgun houses where my wrestling buddy lived, no garden came close to matching ours. I never missed a meal, but I doubt if my wrestling buddy was so fortunate. He may well have been hungry even as we wrestled. The question arose in my mind: "What if our economic circumstances had been reversed, then whose shoulders would have been pinned?"

Perhaps even more haunting: In 1936 my companion may have been aware that in those days he was not supposed to win. After all, there wasn't just segregation, there was also intimidation (not just in the south, of course) so, even if he felt he could win, did he at some point, simply let up, let me win as I was supposed to do?

There were rare athletic exceptions in the blacks vs. whites world. The two I remember most vividly were Joe Louis in boxing and Jesse Owens in Olympic track and field. Both were heavyweight champions in their sports.

Today the segregation and intimidation of that earlier day are all but gone. The wrestling mat and the playing field are level.

A GARDEN OF SONG

Wilson Van Buren was a black man who plowed our garden every spring while I was growing up in Phenix City. (He was called "colored" then — we're talking 1920s and 1930s).

He would bring his mule to the garden in early spring and break up the ground, lay it off for planting, preparing it so that I (upon getting old enough) could cart cow manure from the barn and spread it in the rows, then plant cabbage, onion buttons, sweet potato slips and put down corn, beans, peas and other seeds.

After three or four weeks, Wilson would plow the rows of veggies, loosening the soil near the growing plants, getting rid of a lot of weeds and grass that reduced the amount of my hoeing.

Our garden was not small. Plowing took Wilson three or four hours or longer. Although he was preparing the garden for my labor, and that of other family members, I did not particularly relish gardening. Nonetheless I have fond memories of his singing as he worked. He had a strong, rich voice, very appealing, and he could be heard a city block away. As I remember, his songs were all hymns. I'm sure that on Sundays he thrilled the hearts of many churchgoers during their worship services.

Wilson's hymns revealed his lifestyle; perhaps I should say his lifestyle was not inconsistent with that of a man who so joyfully sang gospel numbers.

My father died in November 1938, and I don't remember our family ever having another garden. In the springs of 1939, 1940 and 1941 (before I entered the Army), I was busy in school and actually away from home in 1940 and 1941, so the spring of 1938 must have been the last time I heard Wilson sing.

I saw him only once after he last sang in our garden. He was on his deathbed. I don't recall the month or year, but I was home a few days from college and Mama told me Wilson was ill.

When I visited him, the weather was warm, all windows and doors in his house were wide open. His bedroom was neat but flies were numerous and a nuisance. There were no screens. I would estimate that Wilson was 60 years old. He was worn out, too weak to talk. I can't say that he acknowledged me, but his wife, though heavily burdened, was quietly friendly.

Soon Wilson was gone, and I sensed that an era was passing. In our part of the world, only a few plowmen would be walking behind mules. There were certainly none who could sing like Wilson.

READER AND TEACHER

When I was an early teenager, my father's eyesight grew dim and I began reading the newspaper to him. Once in a while he would become irritated with me because my enunciation was not clear. Typical teen, mumbling and jumbling.

"Re-read that sentence"..."What was that?"... "Come again?"... "Not so fast"...etc. Those comments I know now were indications I could have done better.

I was a good reader in one sense. Words came easy for me, I didn't hem and haw trying to figure out how to pronounce a word. My problem simply was not enunciating clearly.

I caught on somewhat, I think, so that perhaps toward the end I read better than in the beginning. I don't suppose that it dawned on me that my father was quietly, patiently (generally speaking) teaching me to speak with clarity and with good diction.

Furthermore, little did I ever dream that when my father was pushing me to speak clearly that someday I would be a client mouthpiece, would make hundreds of speeches and, as of this writing, spend 43-plus years teaching law students and serve 50 years teaching Sunday School. (Sunday School efforts continue.)

Suppose I had it all to do over. I think that I would pay closer attention to my father's comments and would try hard to read better.

Who knows? Teenagers really lean toward doing their own things. Ask my four children.

MAMA'S BOY

After a brief illness my father died November 4, 1938, at our Phenix City home. He was 86: I was a 17-year-old high school senior. We had lived in Phenix City since 1924.

I was nearly 3 and sister Bernice (Nena) close to 2 when Mama and Papa moved from Morristown, Tennessee, to Phenix City in the spring or summer of 1924, shortly before brother Andrew arrived in August. Brother David was born in June 1928 and that was two months before my future wife, Patti Mullins, was born in Helena, Alabama.

Age 17- 1939

My parents' move from Tennessee to Alabama was prompted by economic reasons. Mama owned 40 acres in Phenix City and Papa, a retired wholesale grocer, had some cash. So, pooling their resources, they built our home place, at least 10 rental houses, and bought three others.

I recall that when Papa died, Mama was left with eight rental houses and our home place, all paid for. The Depression was still bitter, as it was during most of the 1930s, yet the rental income would sustain Mama for 19 years, the remainder of her life.

The Friday Papa died I came in from school about 3:00 p.m. Mama was standing just inside the front screen door. She was sniffing slightly. Sensing what had happened, I said, "Papa's gone."

Watery-eyed, she hugged me and said softly, "Son, you are now the man of the house."

I remember that on the one hand I was honored by my mother's confidence in me (which she periodically expressed), on the other hand I believed myself unworthy at 17, not ready for such a role.

In May, following Papa's death in November, 69 of us graduated from Central High School.

Early June, I left home with Mama's blessing and that of her three younger children to attend Southern Union Junior College at Wadley, Alabama. The new "man of the house" never again spent more than a month at home on a visit to Phenix City.

During the summer of 1941, Mama and her brood moved to Birmingham. She paid $3,500 cash for a newly remodeled house directly across the street from Howard College where I had enrolled in 1940. I soon moved from the Lambda Chi Alpha fraternity house and lived in Mama's new home until I enlisted in the army on May 13, 1942.

One might think that Mama moved to Birmingham to be near her "man of the house". Fact is, with three other children to educate, living near the campus in East Lake appealed to her as a good investment because her children all could live at home while getting a college education.

Mama's decision to move was clearly based on economics. Although her plan was a good one, it was altered by America's entry into World War II. By the war's end all four of Mama's children had left home to join the war effort.

During the war I was fortunate to have the opportunity as a pilot to fly home and visit Mama on a number of weekends. She was always upbeat and brave, a valiant lady indeed!

She did not need me to be man of the house. I was always "Mama's boy" and proud of it.

LONG-LASTING GIFT

A Bible I have is actually a small New Testament dated February 1, 1934. The little book was given to me at my baptism (translated, my "sprinkling") on that date in the Pilgrim Congregational Church in Phenix City.

I attended Pilgrim until high school graduation at age 17. In June I left Phenix City for Southern Union Junior College at Wadley, Alabama, and while there visited other churches.

During my freshman year I read all the New Testament, then the Old. Beyond a doubt, this was my most significant accomplishment my first year in college.

However, I now consider it a significant accomplishment not to have lost or misplaced my "little Bible", my baptismal New Testament, which I have had in my possession until this day. The little Book carries the following words on the inside cover: "Believing the Lord Jesus Christ died for me, I now accept Him as my Savior, my Lord, and my King: and by His grace I will live for Him day by day."

These words are followed by my signature and date February 1, 1934. More than 75 years later I still gladly subscribe to this testimony.

_____

Frank W. Donaldson   February 1, 2010

MODEL LOVE AFFAIR

Early in boyhood I assembled my first model airplane; the love affair lasted all my life. I do not recall whether that first one was a flying model or a stationary (hard) one. I built both kinds, always from kits.

Air shows were held at the nearby Columbus, Georgia, airport, within easy walking distance from our home in Phenix City. As a child I really fell in love with airplanes, and that love either began or was enhanced at the air shows.

However, one year I was within a few hundred feet of a stunt-plane crash. The pilot had attempted to perform an Immelmann (half-loop) on takeoff when the plane stalled and plunged into the ground so close to me I could smell the pilot's burning flesh as he perished in the plane before my eyes. I went home ill and did not touch a model plane for about two years. At age 14 I went back to it, building mostly flying models.

I would fly each model until it crashed. Sometimes after spending hours or even days building one, I would torch it and watch it fly while aflame, crash and burn. Nonsensical? Perhaps, perhaps not. I learned a lot about the aspect of flight and imagined how I would escape a plane in various kinds of trouble. Most important, I learned that planes are delicate and fragile; that it's easy for one to go awry in the air or even on the ground. No doubt about it, I would later become a better pilot through my experience with model airplanes.

At 15 I entered a model plane "flight contest" at the Columbus Airport. I don't recall the sponsor, but the contest was in the summer of 1937 (I was 16 that Sept. 8).

My model, with a huge wing-tip span, won third prize, losing to two smaller models that stayed aloft a few seconds longer than mine.

I enjoy telling about winning third place because I won the prize I would have chosen among the top three. I liked to fish and my prize was a rod and reel that suited me to a "T," just what I wanted and didn't own until then. Until that day my boyhood fishing had been with cane poles, crickets and worms. The rod and reel put me in silver water; now I could use artificial lures if I chose.

Truth is I still enjoy fishing with a cane pole, especially for bream.

TANGLING WITH A FENCE

A recent accident I had while playing tennis required surgery. I was hurt in a way only a man can appreciate. This reminded me of childhood buddy Doug Blanton's encounter with a barbed wire fence.

Doug and I were in our early teens in Phenix City. He and five other boys in the neighborhood, all of us close to the same age, engaged in various fun activities: shooting marbles (Mama never let me play "for keeps"); cops, robbers and Indians using homemade rubber guns; kite-flying; baseball; hide-and-seek; tree-climbing; swinging on vines; swimming in Holland Creek; fishing; hunting and trapping. Depression-era boys engaged in these activities across the land. Many of our good times together took place in the woods and pastureland owned by my parents.

My father had put three or four strands of barbed wire around 40 acres to keep our cows nearby. Seldom did a cow escape through his well-built fence. I still remember how tightly Papa drew each strand between the posts.

On one occasion Doug and I were playing in the cow pasture, unaccompanied by any other pals, when Doug decided he could and would jump the nearby fence. He got a good running start, getting his whole body over the top strand—well almost. A barb snagged his private parts, causing a considerable tear.

We kids were taught not to swear. Doug did a good job holding his tongue, at the same time holding his private parts with both hands.

Cuts and bruises were treated in our locale in the 1930s with either Mercurochrome, iodine or kerosene—sometimes a combination. For example, a bruise with a cut might get a touch of kerosene on the bruise and iodine or Mercurochrome on the cut.

As a kid I put iodine on a wound, although it added to the pain. Agony from the iodine was brief and I had great confidence in the anti-infection and healing value. It always worked.

Spurning iodine, Doug hurried home for treatment.

Doug's dad was a carpenter, but not much building was taking place, so the Blantons had to closely watch every penny. Times were especially difficult for them, so I doubt if Doug ever saw a doctor. The family depended upon nonprescription medicine, and I don't think Doug ever got a tetanus shot.

The money crunch also meant that Doug probably received a stern lecture from his mother for tearing his pants. Doing anything that might shorten the life of a pair of trousers or overalls was looked upon with parental disapproval.

Years later a news item revealed that Phenix City had a police detective named Doug Blanton. Detective Blanton had been on the force a number of years when I read in a newspaper that he had been discharged after socking the mayor on the chin during an argument.

I was disappointed but not necessarily surprised. After all, if this was my teenage buddy who had picked a 4½ foot barbed wire fence to hurdle he just might someday sock his boss. On the other hand, my friend, Doug, was a bright, top-quality lad.

Papa's Promise

The highboy has been in our family many hundreds of years. I'd say no less than 300. I've had it since Mama died in 1957. Papa had it from his youth in the 1800s.

Thirty years ago, my wife Patti refinished the highboy (which most people know is a high chest of drawers mounted on legs). I informed her not long afterwards, "Your refinishing job has cost us $50,000." I don't recall whether she grimaced or chuckled an, "Oh, sure, ha-ha."

My remark had been prompted by my recently having heard that antique experts put a great deal more value on such items when they are "grungy". Removing the grunge substantially reduces an antique's value.

After Patti made the highboy spic and span, its worth probably was reduced to no more than $75,000. Tough luck! Some days are better than others.

However, I do not wish for Patti to

despair; the piece is made of rosewood, so perhaps if it is kept in the family another 300 years it will again be grungy and have great worth to her progeny. I'm sure twice-grungy will make the thing invaluable.

But there is more to this story than an antique's grunge. A few days ago while I was downstairs where we keep the highboy, I glanced at the top-left drawer, at which time I recalled Papa's cigars, his booze and the promise he first made me when I was about 10 or 11.

The highboy stands 6 feet, 5 inches on four sturdy, decorative feet (adding 7 inches to its height) and contains nine drawers. The lower four drawers are 37 inches wide, same width as the antique; two drawers above them are each 18 inches wide; three top drawers are parallel and each 11 inches wide.

All drawers have meticulously carved wooden handles. Each drawer opens and closes easily; the top left drawer automatically locks when pushed shut. In it Papa kept a box containing his cigars. Now and then when he was given cigars, he promptly locked them in his "secret" place. We kids knew about them because once in a while Papa had a smoke and a toddy. We knew of his covert activity because we peeped.

In the drawer with his cigars Papa kept a bottle of whiskey. What kind and where he got it during prohibition I never had an idea.

During most of my early boyhood years prohibition was the law of the land. Well, that was not always applicable to Phenix

City where we lived. Reportedly you could buy any illicit thing in and around the gambling joints on the west bank of the Chattahoochee River (the Alabama side) near the 14th Street bridge. But if I were a gambler I'd bet my last penny that Papa never went in one of those places.

Nevertheless, he possessed his bottle and periodically (not often) he took a drink he referred to as "my toddy."

After I became a teenager, Papa told me that while he was a young man he had a toddy more often than he did when he grew older. But I suspect that he would have taken nips more often had he not been aware of the importance of good fatherly qualities. No doubt that curtailed his use of the stuff.

I'm glad that family records disclose that Papa's thirst for toddies was reduced by a preacher's strong message. He was then in his twenties. After that message, he locked the bottle and his toddy cup in the highboy's top left drawer. That drawer could be opened only by pulling out the drawer directly beneath, reaching into the open drawer and pushing up a flexible sliver of wood that let the upper drawer be opened.

One day when I saw Papa standing at the highboy sniffing a cigar, he made me this promise: "If you don't smoke or drink or chew tobacco until you're 21, I'll give you a gold watch and chain." At the time I probably was in the fifth or sixth grade. That promise was renewed as I entered the experimental teen years.

I'll leave it to the reader as to whether I became entitled to the gold watch and chain. Three or four times during my junior high years I smoked rabbit tobacco, nothing more than an impotent weed. Neither of my parents was concerned about the rabbit tobacco becoming habit-forming. Actually it's so insipid that perhaps parents should encourage smoking rabbit tobacco as a way of turning youngsters from smoking stronger stuff.

As a new teenager I also smoked part of a real cigarette without my parent's knowledge. I also took a chew of tobacco — yuck! And in my freshman year of college, age 18, I puffed a whole cigar. Sick? Was I ever!! So nauseated that I've never wanted to try another.

Cigarettes were no strong temptation to me for two reasons. My close buddies in high school didn't smoke, so there was no peer pressure. More importantly, even if I had been tempted, I didn't have the money to buy cigarettes. My 15 cents a week, mostly from my parents, was always used for a Saturday western and popcorn or peanuts at the local cinema.

As for drink, I never touched it. To this day I've never tasted beer; I can't stand the smell of it. Once, past age 21, I took a sip of bourbon, didn't like either the taste or odor, so that was that.

In the early years of our marriage, Patti and I had many opportunities to imbibe, as I had had in the military, but at the expense of being called fuddy-duddies, or worse, we have stayed with colas even at parties.

We would have preferred that our soft drinks be served in bottles, but those were not chilled so we accepted them served in glasses with ice, which I'm sure made us appear to be sipping our libation. At times we probably appeared to be misfits at a "social hour". In later years socializers don't seem to give a second thought when alcoholic cocktails are declined. Perhaps a host thinks the refusal results from a problem one has with strong drink; it's known that former heavy drinkers mustn't take even a small drink of alcohol.

In any event Patti and I are not bugged about the matter as we once were. Have attitudes changed? Or have my wife and I simply become known as teetotalers or just hopeless snobs? Surely not the latter.

Back to Papa's offer: Had he lived until I was 21, would the watch and chain have been rightfully mine? Only one cigarette, one cigar, one tobacco chew! Or did he intend to convey to me that if I never developed a *habit* for tobacco and alcohol before age 21, I had earned fulfillment of his promise?

I read recently that a study had been completed in which the scholars had determined that if a person did not smoke or drink before age 21, that person is not likely ever to develop a habit for either. Perhaps my father knew that more than 70 years ago. Wonder what accounts for Papa and the scholars both choosing age 21 as the magic number?

Papa died when I was 17 so that the question of my entitlement to the watch and chain became moot — or did it? He never mentioned it in his will. Was that intentional or did he forget to make the "bequest"?

He could have left the decision to Mama, executrix of his will. Had he done so, should Mama have honored Papa's promise?

Mama knew that someday the highboy was to be mine and that I was not likely to use the lock-drawer to secrete booze or tobacco. Isn't that what Papa really had in his thoughts when he made me that promise?

LAZY EYE

A Columbus, Georgia, optometrist prescribed glasses for me when I was 16 or 17. What a rip off! I was the last kid in town who needed glasses. In later years, Dr. N.E. Miles, a renowned Birmingham eye specialist, told me that my eyes were among the five best pair he had ever examined.

Why a visit to the Columbus eye man? For several days I had had a headache — most unusual for me to have such a problem, that is, unless I ate chocolate candy or drank a few too many cups of hot chocolate. Even then the chocolate meant a headache would follow for only a few hours. No chocolate, no headache. Why this one lingered I never knew.

Thinking perhaps my eyes were the cause I wasted some of my parent's money buying glasses I never needed.

Until this day I think the doc should have leveled with me, telling me my eyesight was really top-notch, that I could see like a hawk. Had he suggested I visit an M.D. to diagnose the headache he would have earned the same fee. Well, that is, unless he also sold glasses. I don't recall whether he did.

Nonetheless, I came out ahead. The visit was clearly worthwhile; no, it was invaluable. The exam revealed my left eye was lazy. The examiner had me look at the lead of a sharpened #2 pencil held some 8 to 10 inches in front of my eyes. He moved the pencil to within 3 to 4 inches of my nose, then away from it 10 to 12 inches. He made a figure 8 with the pencil point, first one way, and then the other and he watched my eyes. He noticed my left eye was not following the pencil lead, the right eye was doing so. He then taught me how to detect that I had a lazy eye — and what to do about it: I held the pencil near my face and moved it as he had done, first toward my eyes, away from them, and followed that with the figure 8s. While engaging in these exercises in his presence, I put a hand periodically over my right eye. He asked, "Was your left eye looking at the pencil lead?"

"No." The eye had to refocus its point of concentration. The shifting of my viewing area was noticeable. Placing a hand over my left eye revealed the right eye was closely following the pencil lead for each exercise.

The next day I began my daily exercise program at home, a minute or two in the morning and likewise in the evening.

I was faithful to the doc's recommended regime so that after a few weeks my eye ceased being so lazy- to the extent I could depend on it to closely follow the pencil lead.

A few years later this all paid off in a distinctly positive way during my Army Air Force cadet eye test. A lazy eye would have been observed and blocked my pilot training. Those exercises made the eye exam a breeze.

Nearly seven decades after I began training the lazy eye not to do its own thing, it nonetheless continues its tendency to lapse back into laziness, always has. Exercise brings it back into focus.

I still have excellent vision, 20/20 with glasses. But I must not overlook doing my eye routine.

At 1604 21st Street, Phenix City, Alabama – where Frank lived, age 3-17

Snow at Southern Union Junior College,
Wadley, Alabama-January 6, 1940

JUNIOR COLLEGIAN

*Mama visited me at Southern Union Junior College
after I had been away from home 30 days, my longest
ever. Was I homesick! Never was I so glad to see her.
She was a beautiful sight.*

PINCHING PENNIES, SPENDING DOLLARS

When in 1939 I enrolled as a freshman in Southern Union Junior College at Wadley, Alabama, the school was owned by the Congregational Church. For years before and after, Southern Union clung to life by pinching every penny possible that came its way from a few contributors.

President and Mrs. Ross Ensminger lived in a modest house on campus. Every year the president traveled to the northeastern U.S. where the Congregationalist Church was strong, trying to raise money to keep Southern Union afloat. Each year he succeeded, barely.

I showed up in early June 1939 and earned tuition, room and board by working for the school for 15 cents an hour. My work centered on a large garden, a couple of milk cows, ditch-digging and the like.

A large outdoor, wood-burning furnace heated the men's dorm and the furnace got a lot of my attention. Outside work took most of my time and energy.

Inside the campus buildings, those of us on "work scholarships" stayed busy cleaning, painting, dishwashing, etc. None of us ever saw a penny; all earnings were "applied."

The academic-year scholarship called for either three months full-time summer work or part-time work during semesters. Opting for summer work meant that I did not work during the regular school year, September through May. Thus I had no excuse for not studying diligently. Even so, I did not study hard.

After my freshman year, my grades, though weak, were transferable to Howard College. I should have been embarrassed because in high school I had made mostly A's.

Of the 150 or so students enrolled at Southern Union in the 1939-40 school year, several dozen were coeds. I cannot blame my less-than-excellent grades on the coeds, although I took a special liking to one of them. Nothing came of it.

I write of Southern Union 68 years after the big snow. It was an especially big snow to me because I had never seen snow on the ground, only a few falling flakes. During my boyhood days in Phenix City we were snowless. I still have Brownie camera photos of the big snow at Southern Union.

It was January 1940 and Southern Union had more than deep snow; the school was in deep poverty. We were still in the throes of the Great Depression; only World War II would relieve that plight. The economic tragedy took its toll on millions of individuals and institutions like Southern Union were sorely plagued by it.

The college was so poor the professor of French, a bachelor, lived in the men's dorm, and a woman professor lived in the women's dorm. I'm sure that neither had a salary sufficient for monthly home payments or rent.

For years Southern Union continued to operate with its small enrollment; the president and his father continued to search for college operating funds. I recall that 10 years after my time on campus, Fred Ensminger, the president's father, contacted me seeking funds for the college. He expressed gracious thanks for my $25 check.

In the 1960s, with Southern Union Junior College in financial straits, the state of Alabama purchased it. Money flowed in for the first time in the school's history. Old buildings were dismantled and new ones constructed. A dam was built and a lake created.

A few miles from Wadley at Lafayette, a branch campus was established. Enrollment soared. College personnel were paid decently.

Since my days on the S.U. campus, many colleges across the country have folded their tents or merged with other schools.

Although some institutions of higher education struggle today to make ends meet, I doubt that in any college two fulltime professors reside in a dormitory because their school can't pay them their due, as was the case at Southern Union.

WHEN OLD IS YOUNG

Floy Gunter was 18. So was I. We were in the freshman class at Southern Union Junior College at Wadley, Alabama, in the 1939-40 academic year.

Floy, a pretty brunette, and I became good friends. Sometimes on a walk we held hands, but although we liked each other, the relationship never got serious.

Therefore, it was not a bit surprising to learn that she was fond of a man who lived near her home in Milton, Florida. I recall that fondness, not because she mentioned him so much, but because he was 28 years old. At the time I was baffled that an 18-year-old co-ed could be interested in such an ancient person.

Little did I realize at that time how really young 28 is; that I would be that age when Patti and I married. Even so, I am only seven years older than my wife, not 10, as was the case with Floy and her back-home beau.

I left Southern Union after one year and have not seen Floy since 1940. I did hear that she married the "old" guy.

HOWARD COLLEGE, PRE-WAR

My major accomplishment at Howard
before World War II: Learning to fly.
The course could have been entitled Piper Cub 101.

JOEL AND MAE, ROOM AND BOARD

Joel and Mae Appleby, "Uncle Joel and Aunt Mae," made me an offer in the spring of 1940 that I could not refuse. They told me I could live in their Birmingham home rent-free the following college year.

Frank Donaldson
March -1942

Uncle Joel was Mama's brother. He and Aunt Mae had no children. This explains in part why they made the generous offer.

Though Joel and Mae were Baptists, they made clear that I was free to attend either Birmingham Southern, a Methodist school, or Howard College, Baptist. They lived much closer to Birmingham-Southern. Their home at 2318 Avenue I in Ensley was only a 15 or 20 minute trolley ride and walk to Southern, whereas Howard was a full one-hour trolley ride, plus a short walk to the trolley line, plus the inevitable wait for the trolley.

A trolley (streetcar) ran on Avenue I in front of the Appleby home, a block in front of Ensley High School, but I seldom rode it. Almost always there was a long wait for that trolley, then a transfer to another one. So I walked to where I could board trolley No. 38. Trolleys were powered by overhead power lines; the 60-minute trip to Howard was 7 cents.

At the time of Joel and Mae's offer, I was a freshman at Southern Union Junior College and very much interested in attending a four-year institution. Either Birmingham-Southern or Howard would have been a good choice; each was an inviting opportunity.

Mother was a Methodist and would have been pleased had I enrolled at Southern. However, she sincerely wanted me to choose the college I deemed to be in my best interest.

Howard business manager, Lent Brewster, told me I could work for the college all summer for 30 cents an hour. The earnings would be applied to my tuition. The previous summer's earnings of 15 cents an hour had been applied to tuition and room and board at Southern Union. Brewster's offer was too attractive for me to turn down, so I chose Howard College.

After painting our white frame house in Phenix City the first week of June 1940, I yielded to a yen for travel. Doug Blanton, a Phenix City buddy, and I headed west, hitchhiking. We spent our first night in an old rundown motel on the outskirts of Montgomery on U.S. Highway 80. We shared a room for 25 cents each. Luckily there were no bedbugs, at least none found us.

The next morning I mentioned to Doug that I should check my summer work schedule with Mr. Brewster at Howard to see when he expected me to report. So instead of heading on west, we thumbed north toward Birmingham on U.S. 31.

That afternoon I visited Mr. Brewster, who encouraged me to begin campus work pronto. Naturally Doug was disappointed (big time) that our trip west was abandoned. I explained that I badly needed money for tuition, so he headed back to Phenix City.

Then I proceeded to Uncle Joel's and Aunt Mae's house, where I was given the front bedroom as my own.

Uncle Joel worked the early shift at U.S. Steel's nearby TCI plant, so he and Aunt Mae were up at 5 a.m. Mae served us breakfast each workday morning. Breakfast was my only meal with them the year I spent there.

I never heard of Aunt Mae and Uncle Joel ever having anyone live with them except me.

Uncle Joel died in 1948, seven years after I moved from their home to the Lambda Chi Alpha fraternity house on the Howard College campus. Mae moved to Phenix City near relatives and died a few years later.

Almost 60 years after I lived in their home, the son of a niece of mine applied for admission to Cumberland Law School at Samford University. As the young man needed financial aid, and as our children were in homes of their own, Patti and I offered him a rent-free room in our place, only a four-minute commute to the law school. But it was not to be; he was not accepted for admission.

For a number of years after our children left home Patti and I had no one live with us. Then in recent years three of our children and their families had need for a spot to land during their house transitions. On each of these occasions we opened our home to them; for months they were our guests. We enjoyed them all, without exception. Each one brought back to me memories of Uncle Joel and Aunt Mae.

TESTED, COMING UP SHORT

About the first of October 1940, while a sophomore at Howard College, I enrolled in the federal government-sponsored Civilian Pilot Training Program. Ground school and flight training were at the Municipal Airport in Birmingham.

Only a month earlier I had undergone an appendectomy in Columbus, Georgia, and had spent eight days in the hospital, thus I was still puny when the course began. But 19-year-olds snap back, so I was able to start the course, even if inauspiciously.

After a few days in ground school, we were given a 50-question exam. A correct answer for each multiple-choice question was worth two points; each wrong answer brought a two-point deduction.

Each of us graded another student's paper. My total grade was four! That meant I had missed 48 of the 50 answers. A few days later the instructor spoke to me about my performance. I recall that he said I really had not done badly on the exam and that I should not be discouraged. Then he added, perhaps in partial explanation: "The student who graded your paper last week has flunked out."

I had no further ground school problems.

COLUMBIANA, LOST AND FOUND

During my civilian pilot training in 1940 my instructor pilot was Chad Bridges. He was tough talking, big, and towered over me. I was 19 years old, 5 feet 7 inches and weighed 125 pounds. But Bridges liked me, I think. Once in a while he would grunt some sign of approval or demonstrate it another way.

For example, we students were required to take a solo "cross-country" flight: Birmingham to Bessemer to Columbiana and return. We were instructed to get someone at each airport to sign a form stating that we had landed there.

Upon my return to the Birmingham Municipal Airport I informed Mr. Bridges that I had not landed at Columbiana because

I couldn't find it. After uttering a couple of vituperative epithets, the instructor insisted that I was mistaken, that I had found Columbiana. "Give me that paper," he snapped and forged a name on my form. Tapping his index finger on the name he had signed, he snarled, "That Shelby (County) farmer swears you landed there!"

After years of flying, I've yet to land in Columbiana — except on that paper.

Once during a training flight I told Mr. Bridges I didn't like his rough language, especially when he gave me a hard time while we were in the air. "What are you going to do about it?" he yelled above the engine noise. I replied that I was tempted to take the cotter pin out of the joystick and hit him over the head with the stick. That really set him off, but it wouldn't be appropriate here to quote his precise words. I do recall his saying that if I tried to hit him, he would undo his control stick, turn around (he sat in front), and beat me over the head with it. That would have been a difficult trick as he practically filled up the front of the plane and couldn't have turned around.

Thank goodness we were just letting off steam. Picture the two of us without a control stick —even a Piper Cub wouldn't put up with that!

In the government's civilian pilot training course, before they could solo, students were required to have eight hours dual instruction. So when I got my eight hours, Mr. Bridges said I was ready and turned me loose.

I'll never forget that first solo flight. One reason: Mr. Bridges weighed 220 pounds and when both of us were aboard, it seemed to me that little plane would never lift off the ground. On my solo when I opened the throttle, the little Cub lifted off almost like a helicopter. My first solo was otherwise uneventful.

For the record, I should note that all our takeoffs and landings were on grass. We did not use the concrete runways.

In January 1941 I got my private pilot's license. I then did something Mama would not have approved. I bought a fifth of scotch (or was it bourbon?) and gave it to instructor Bridges. Perhaps he had suggested the gift; he probably suggested it. The purchase at the state store was the last and only time I spent money for booze.

THE PILOT WHO COULDN'T DRIVE

In 1940 Wendell Givens, my editor for most of this book, was a freshman and I was a sophomore at Howard College in Birmingham. We became friends at Howard and remained good buddies. He passed away in 2006.

A few years ago Wendell retired from The Birmingham News where he had worked many years. He had spent four and a half decades in the newspaper business after college. All of which has little to do, other than background, with what follows.

In January 1941, soon after I had earned a pilot's license, I had an opportunity to take a friend for a flight. With only a private pilot's license I could not charge a fee, so all my flights were at my expense. But it cost no more for me to rent a Piper Cub and haul a passenger than to rent a plane and fly alone. "Like a plane ride, Wendell?" He would. His first. We flew over Birmingham and environs.

Years later Wendell recalled that he clearly remembered every aspect of that flight, especially one over the First Avenue viaduct. "You banked sharply over Sloss Furnace," he said, "and I looked straight down into those red blazes." He didn't care for that view. "Move away," he yelled over the Cub's noisy engine. Wendell didn't appear nervous, but he must have thought that, in the unlikely event the plane went down, there were more suitable places. We circled Sloss two or three more minutes before heading back to the airport.

After landing without incident, we walked to First Avenue North and thumbed a ride to town. We were given a lift by a man we'd never seen before, but he must have guessed we wouldn't make trouble. Near a downtown intersection he double-parked and told us, "I've got to run in this store a minute. If you see a policeman headed this way, one of you young men slide under the wheel and drive around the block. I'll be ready to go by then."

We replied in unison, "Yes sir." But as soon as our driver was out of earshot, Wendell said, "That will have to be you. I don't drive." I had to 'fess up. "I don't drive either."

Wendell looked at me in total surprise. "What do you mean you don't drive? You just flew me over this city, and you can't drive a car?"

"You heard me. You should know poor boys don't own cars."

Wendell accepted that bit of logic (I think), but he pressed the point. "You don't own an airplane either, but you just flew one," still shaking his head in disbelief.

Fortunately no policeman arrived and our driver soon returned, none the wiser.

WORKING AWAY FROM HOME

As related earlier, I worked the summer of 1939 at Southern Union Junior College, and during the summer of 1940 I worked on campus at Howard College in Birmingham. In early June I moved in with Uncle Joel and Aunt Mae Appleby in Ensley.

Some things really changed in the summer of 1941. I worked for TCI, a division of U.S. Steel, at the Wenonah iron ore plant between Birmingham and Bessemer.

There I earned 55 cents an hour and was paid real money. That made it possible for me to live on campus at Howard. I had joined the Lambda Chi Alpha fraternity and lived in the frat house, having meals at Mrs. Stevens' "hash house" across Fourth Avenue South from the campus. Mrs. Stevens served excellent meals country style. A bunch of students sat around a big table and passed food to one another and we helped our plates from bowls.

I was 19 and making money. Trolley fare was 7 cents and a movie cost a quarter. I rode to work and back with fellow student R. Wheeler Flemming in his car for a nominal charge.

A good meal was 35 cents at Walgreen's Drug Store downtown. I learned about that at Easter time while selling shoes at Kinney's shoe store on Second Avenue North. My commission was 5 percent. I ate lunch at Walgreen's for about two weeks during that employment.

The most expensive shoes at Kinney's were $4, which, obviously, made my commission 20 cents. Most shoes were $2, thus earning me a dime. This meant I had to sell two pair to make trolley fare and five pair to commute and have lunch.

This was valuable growing-up experience for a 19-year-old. I remember the store manager patting me on the back with a "Well done!" when I sold a pair of the $4 shoes. Think how I would have been in clover if I had been paid a 10 percent commission instead of 5!

As related next in "Rookie Weatherman," I was paid real money for several months in late 1941 and early 1942 just before enlisting in the U.S. Army Air Forces. It sure beat shoveling iron ore and selling shoes.

ROOKIE WEATHERMAN

In the latter part of 1941 while a junior at Howard College, I latched onto a dream job with the U.S. Department of Commerce in its Weather Bureau at the Birmingham Airport.

I don't recall the actual name of the position, but I was a "weatherman". My predecessor had vacated the position and I was placed in his slot. I think he probably left for military duty, as I soon would do.

When I learned there was an opening, I jumped at it. The assignment was an eight-hour shift mostly at night. The pay was especially good for a 20-year-old and there was ample "free" time to study, time that I used wisely — well, some nights.

The job called for me to report current weather conditions and make forecasts. To do this, each hour I would send aloft a helium-filled balloon and track it with a theodolite, an instrument to help determine wind direction and velocity at 1,000-foot levels. Of course, such determinations were limited by visibility, which sometimes was hindered by fog, smog or clouds.

In clear, cloudless weather, the balloon, about the size of an average ripe watermelon, was soon out of sight. With a low overcast the balloon quickly disappeared into the clouds, giving a very limited wind reading. The low clouds at times prevented my obtaining the wind velocity as high as 1,000 feet above the airport. However, when there were overcast clouds (solid layer) and the balloon was still visible until it disappeared into them, the height of the clouds could be determined and put on my report.

At night I put a lighted candle in a clear, enclosed container and fastened the container to the bottom of the balloon. The light was followed through the theodolite until it either entered a cloud or went out into the night sky beyond my vision. Winds aloft at 1,000-foot levels and cloud ceilings were thus determined even in darkness.

I also reported rainfall, measured by a gauge on the roof, just outside the second floor, near where I stood with the theodolite. A few feet over was the thermometer that was read hourly.

Gathering all the required data took me about 10 minutes out of each hour; thus, the study time. A Teletype promptly sent the information to other weather stations across the country. This served at least two purposes: real weathermen could collect data from many stations and use it to help make their forecasts. Also, pilots would call or visit the weather stations and read the data from stations along their scheduled route, as well as the one at their destination and others nearby, to make appropriate flight plans and to know reasonably well what weather to expect.

Occasionally a pilot's flight plan had to be altered substantially due to existing or anticipated poor weather on his planned route. Birmingham and other cities occasionally would get "socked in," especially in winter with low clouds or fog. When this occurred at the Birmingham airport, although it is 610 feet above sea level, aircraft — commercial and private — were not permitted to take off or land. The airfield simply was closed to air traffic.

As rudimentary as were the procedures for gathering weather data, the reports helped significantly to give pilots a reasonably good idea of the kind of weather they would encounter. The "weathermen" mostly were in the business of promoting safety for pilots, their crews, and passengers.

I became a fair-to-middling forecaster and sometimes, quite good. For example, if the temperature in, say, January at Des Moines, Iowa, was zero at midnight and there was a strong northwest wind, if the temperature in St. Louis at the same hour was 15 degrees with a brisk northwest wind, and if the temperature in Memphis was 22 degrees with a similarly strong northwest wind then I could reasonably forecast a front in Birmingham near daybreak, with even colder weather the next night.

Of course, there were times when a strong south wind blowing in off the Gulf would stymie a cold front somewhere north of Birmingham, blocking the cold air.

Very soon after the United States declared war on Japan following the attack on Pearl Harbor, I was instructed not to give weather information over the telephone to the public. Thus, my reports were no longer available to housewives who called wanting to know whether they should cover their plants that night, or to golfers wanting to know if rain was likely the next day.

My weather information became available only to persons with a "need to know." Under the new rules, housewives and golfers didn't need to know. The policy excluded John Q. Public from our information. After all, if the information got into the public domain, our military enemies might put it to use. I admit that a rookie like me was baffled as to how the enemy could be helped by my telling a golfer he'd better take an umbrella next morning.

Although my work with the Weather Bureau lasted only a few months, the experience became very helpful to me during World War II. As a pilot I understood how to quickly read and interpret weather maps and reports. I could decide without difficulty whether to fly into a storm. Some storms were penetrable, some not. The former "weatherman" understood.

Was weather forecasting a good job? Ask Tillman Gladney, fellow Howard student who succeeded me in the weather office. Tillman liked the work well enough to make a career as a meteorologist with the Department of Commerce.

MILITARY LIFE

It seems almost sacrilegious to recall that my
World War II life as a pilot was a snap.
But in the service one follows orders,
and my orders kept me in the States.

I BEAT THE DRAFT

On Thursday, May 12, 1942, Mama went with me from our house at 7777 Fourth Avenue South by trolley to Birmingham's Terminal Station. My luggage was light, but I'm sure Mama's heart was heavy. Her oldest son, 20, had beaten the draft by voluntarily enlisting in the U.S. Army. My leaving left three siblings at home, but not for long as war service saw them all depart within the next three years.

Mama had been a widow since

Aviation Cadet - 1942

November 4, 1938. She was 60 years old when she saw me climb aboard a Southern Railway passenger train for Anniston, Alabama, and Fort McClellan. Neither of us knew, of course, when we would be together again. However, 11 months later I returned home, a second lieutenant on a week's leave of absence.

The 11 months had passed quickly for me, but I doubt if Mama and I were on the same fast clock. There hadn't been a phone conversation — too expensive — but we wrote each other regularly (a stamp was 3 cents, remember?).

Mama was faithful to write newsy, encouraging letters. Those

Aviation Cadet
Randolph Field, 1942

letters lifted my spirits, built up my confidence, and just plain made me want to do well, perhaps to make her proud of me. To this day I thank God for her inspiration. Would that I could be as inspirational to my four children.

Mama had a faith in me that I can't adequately describe. I recall her once saying, "You can do anything you set your mind to do." Fantastic exaggeration, but not to Mama. She truly believed in me and pressed that belief indelibly upon me.

The trip from Birmingham to Fort McClellan took a little more than an hour. There I passed the cursory physical exam and on Friday, May 13, 1942, I became a private in the U.S. Army. The next day I shipped out to Fort McPherson at Atlanta. I took written tests there, scoring 132 on the army I.Q. exam.

A few days later a large number of us traveled on a troop train at night to Keesler Field, Biloxi, Mississippi. There I got lucky and lived in the barracks, not "tent city" (where many, many soldiers were housed), got some shots, drilled, did KP and got a real feel of early army life.

Keesler lasted only a couple of months because I had applied to be an aviation cadet. On July 7, 1942, I was assigned to the Army Air Forces base at San Antonio, Texas.

I soon learned there that competition among cadets would be keen. At Keesler I had participated in a 100-yard dash competing against 100 other privates. I won and the captain wrote Mama a letter of praise, which she shared with me with great parental pride. But at San Antonio we cadets had a 100-yard dash and Mama got no letter. I came in second. I think until this day the cadet who won had better shoes than I did. Also, he had been on his college track team. I had never run track except on my own, sporadically.

Coming in second may have been a good lesson for me. Train, train! Whether the cadet who won that dash ever became a pilot I don't know. But I like to think that if he did fly, I could have outflown him because flying was one thing in which no one could feel more at home than I. Mama would have been pleased.

THE CADET AND FDR

During late summer and the fall of 1942 I was an aviation cadet at Randolph Field, Texas (today Randolph Air Force Base).

I took my first flight September 8, 1942, on my 21st birthday with Lt. Robert Froman. He was a top-quality officer and flight instructor.

On September 19, I first soloed. Lieutenant Froman told me he won three 5-cent Coca-Colas from one of his instructor colleagues because I made several consecutive three-point landings.

Strother Field, Kansas - 1943

Eight days later on September 27, I had a "near" encounter with President Franklin D. Roosevelt. On that beautiful autumn day I was flying solo, practicing various maneuvers when FDR visited Randolph Field. I didn't know that his visit was to take place during my flight, so I was very pleasantly surprised when it occurred with me aloft. As I flew over the perimeter of the field preparing to land, the tower operator told me that I could not do so, and said I should fly in the vicinity of the base until further notice.

I looked down from about 2,000 feet and saw a huge number of Army Air Forces personnel in dress uniform standing at attention on the west ramp. Moving slowly south in front of them was a black convertible with FDR sitting in the back.

I was pleased to extend my flight time and view the ceremonies, albeit from nearly a third of a mile above. As I looked down at the commander-in-chief, I was seeing him for my first and only time. He had visited Columbus, Georgia, when I was a youngster in Phenix City, across the Chattahoochee line. I hadn't attended the parade in Columbus, although the President was within three or four miles of my home.

FDR is not one of my favorite presidents, but I shed a tear on April 12, 1945, when I heard on the radio that he had died. He had been President for 12 years, since I was a boy of 11.

On that fall day in 1942 at Randolph Field I wished that I had had my little 98-cent Brownie camera with me in the BT13 I was flying. I think I could have gotten some magnificent shots. I'm sure the snaps would have been good because I have a beautiful (to me) photo of my alma mater campus, Howard College in Birmingham, that I took with the Brownie in 1941 while flying over the place in a Piper Cub at about 1,500 feet.

2nd Lieutenant, Flight Instructor, Strother Field, KS-1943

Daydreaming now: At Randolph Field I could have buzzed the president and perhaps have given him a great thrill. Of course, my brush with history would have taken a significantly different turn. On December 13, 1942, only 239 of our original cadet class of 400 got their wings and became second lieutenants. If I had given FDR some excitement, there would have been one fewer.

To this day I wonder if the Secret Service had any concern about the president's safety from a nearby flying object piloted by a hotshot cadet with fewer than six hours AAF solo time.

VERTIGO IN THE CLOUDS

The 239 aviation cadets of our 42-X class who graduated on December 13, 1942, at Randolph Field, Texas, were trained especially to become pilot instructors, the only such Army Air Forces cadet class during World War II.

My classmates and I were trained well, notwithstanding a deficiency in one phase of the flight course. The deficiency was not entirely a flight curriculum problem. I refer to the absence of adequate and quality instruments necessary for instrument flying. In other words, although we received some instrument flying instruction, the state of the art

First Lieutenant Donaldson - 1944

for the instruments in those training planes lagged behind the need for flight safety while we were flying in the clouds with the ground not visible.

Our instructors wisely insisted that when we were "flying blind," that is, in the clouds, that we rely solely on the cockpit instruments. We were told to never try flying "by the seat of our pants" when the ground was not visible.

Using cockpit instruments referred to "needle, ball, and airspeed," and use of the compass to the extent feasible.

The cockpit instruments designed to assist the pilot flying in the clouds were embryonic. If the air was turbulent at all, the compass was practically useless. Most of our training planes had no gyrocompasses; understandably because we did aerobatics (loops, snap rolls, spins, etc.) in the same planes we used for instrument flying, and those maneuvers damaged gyroscopes. (Gyroscopes were used in gyrocompasses; these could be coordinated with the compass, and they worked nicely as they did not fluctuate like the compass.)

Flying needle, ball, and airspeed meant that when the pilot could not fly contact (see the ground) but had to rely on his instruments to maintain level flight, it became imperative for him to keep what appeared to be a ball, smaller than a marble, precisely under a little stem called the "needle" and to make sure the needle was vertical. When the plane's wings were not level in flight, the needle was off center, the plane was turning.

As the plane flew through the clouds, the pilot knew his plane was flying straight and level if the needle and ball were centered and the airspeed constant. Constant airspeed indicated the plane nose was neither elevated nor pointed down.

Notwithstanding the paucity of instruments and lack of their sophistication, I learned firsthand how important it was for the pilot to rely completely on the instruments he had before him in the cockpit.

In January 1943, shortly after I arrived in Strother Field, Kansas, from Kelly Field at San Antonio, Texas, I flew at night in my first snow. The air was smooth with no turbulence. When I turned on the landing lights while in the clouds, I was thrilled to see that I was in the heart of a terrific snowstorm. The flakes were huge, thick as hops, and enveloped the aircraft.

When I switched off the landing lights, I concluded that the instruments apparently weren't functioning properly. The needle and ball were centered, the airspeed was at cruising but I sensed that I was turning sharply. Vertigo (dizziness) had hit me, but I didn't realize that it had, so I moved the plane's controls to level it, not believing the instruments' signal that the plane was level and not turning.

Thus, not trusting the instruments, instead now flying by the seat of my pants, I actually began turning the plane. As I pulled back on the stick the airspeed began to build so that very shortly the plane spiraled from the clouds. Underneath the clouds I realized I was in a diving turn.

The snow was falling, but less thick than in the clouds. I could see well enough to orient myself with a few lights visible on the ground and I was able to level the diving BT-13.

Had there not been several hundred feet between the clouds and the ground, Mama would have collected the $10,000 proceeds from my GI life insurance policy with cause of death reported: "airplane crash." More specific cause "vertigo."

I climbed back into the clouds, again into the heavy snow, obeyed the instruments, ignored the vertigo, and soon returned to the airfield having learned an invaluable lesson.

In August I attended instrument flight school at Bryan, Texas, got an "instrument rating," and for several months thereafter taught cadets instrument flying.

Uncertain about the profession or business I might pursue after leaving the service, I also obtained a commercial license before leaving active military service.

From the date of the Kansas snow experience until this day I have believed in an aircraft's cockpit instruments, no matter how tempted I have been to disregard them.

SMUDGE POT AVIATION

In 1943-44 I was a U.S. Army Air Forces pilot instructor of basic training at Strother Field, Kansas, between Winfield and Arkansas City. We taught our cadets not only how to fly at night but also how to fly "cross-country" at night. I quote the term because the flights were a tad short of real cross-country.

We first instructed our young men to shoot landings—to take off and land after dark and fly within view of the air base.

Next was navigation. The cadets would fly a couple of hours between the onset of darkness and midnight on a prescribed route, about 70 to 80 miles on each of three legs.

The training worked thusly: From Strother Field the cadets flew, say, 70 to 80 miles northeasterly, then generally west-southwest about the same flying time, then after a left turn, they returned to the starting place. Or the flight directions might be just the reverse three-leg pattern; in any case, the students got one and a half to two hours night flight time.

Cadets would take off about four to five minutes apart. We instructors sent up a few dozen each evening. Part of these exercises differed from anything one could expect today. However, the method used ensured that the cadets flew their prescribed routes.

They made no landing except upon return to their home base. But the fledgling pilots were required at each of the two turn points to check in by radio with a flight instructor, who was in his plane on the ground. The cadets were to be flying directly above the instructor when the radio call was made.

On occasion, my role was to fly to a designated wheat field, land just before dark, place five smudge pots on the farmer's land and light them. The pots served as a sort of lighted runway for my near-midnight takeoff back to Strother Field.

The particular smudge-pot arrangement was for me to place the first two pots about 20 to 30 yards apart, about 100 or so yards from where the plane was parked; the next two pots about 200 yards farther, 20 to 30 yards apart; the fifth pot another 200 yards away was placed so that I could stand beside it and see the aircraft on a direct line between the other pots.

On takeoff, two lighted smudge pots would be visible on the right side of the plane and two on the left. Shortly before liftoff the lighted pot straight ahead could be seen.

The wheat field was chosen after a low, slow flyover in daylight to make sure there was no hazard (ditch, fence, strung-wire, etc.) to landing in the specified space. The large, flat Kansas wheat fields where the wind blew briskly meant landings and takeoffs were quick and easy to do.

The smudge pots were left behind as a kind of payment to the farmers. If the Army Air Forces made any other deals with the landowners, I was not aware of them.

A cadet flying over the smudge pots used his cockpit mike to contact his instructor, who recorded the cadet's position and flight time. On his return the student pilot reported to the tower.

Flight time would indicate whether a cadet had gotten off course. Getting lost on a clear night was next to impossible. At an altitude of 10,000 feet, a pilot could see 100 miles. Lights on the established, nationally recognized "light line" were 20 miles apart, and I have looked down the line and counted five visible at a time.

Much of this flight training was done after harvest when the ground was firm. Obviously we never used the wheat fields at planting, growing, or harvest time, or when the ground was covered with snow. In those times, small-town airports came in handy except when snowed-in. When snow lay heavy, "cross country" was grounded.

MATAGORDA ISLAND AND THE AFTERMATH

In May 1944, I was still training cadets at Strother Field, Winfield, Kansas, when I had the opportunity to volunteer for combat as a fighter pilot. Another instructor at Strother and I signed up and promptly were transferred to the aerial gunnery school at Matagorda Island, Texas.

I left my 1937 Chevrolet business coupe and fiancée and flew to the Texas coast for two-weeks training prior to leaving for Europe. At Matagorda we flew T6s with 50-caliber machine guns. Our targets were stationary ones on the ground and screens stretched out behind flying T6s.

I shot well and looked forward to air combat over

Strother Field, Kansas - 1943

Germany — until the bad news came. Of the 30 pilots on Matagorda, only half — all captains or majors — were chosen for overseas duty. Among the 15 of us left behind I was a lowly first lieutenant. Worse than being left behind, I was transferred to Aloe

Field near Victoria, about 50 miles from Matagorda, to another cadet flight training school.

After reporting there I was assigned to a squadron where T6s were used for the cadets' advanced training course. Once again I faced the unglamorous labor of flight instructor.

Aloe Field, Texas - 1944

Upon arrival I told the squadron commander that I did not want to be an instructor and had no interest in training cadets. He called the colonel in charge of the flight line and I was ordered to report to him at once.

The colonel wanted to know my problem. I told him that at Strother Field I had volunteered to be a fighter pilot, had left a girl to whom I was engaged, had qualified at Matagorda as an expert in aerial gunnery, and no longer was interested in teaching cadets.

He appeared to understand. "I'm sending you to the base operations officer, Captain Robert Dockstaeder," he told me. "You will be assistant operations officer."

Captain Dockstaeder appeared to be several years older than I was. A combat veteran of the Pacific Theater, soft-spoken and easy-going, he welcomed me. Among other things, he told me the assistant operations officer also was the field lighting officer. Both responsibilities were a cinch.

Handling field lighting was a sergeant with more than 30 years in the service that naturally included World War I. Did he and his crew ever take care of the lights? I don't recall ever seeing a light even flicker, much less burn out!

In early 1945 I jumped at a chance to be temporarily assigned to the Ferry Command. My role was to fly new P51s from Long Beach, California, to Newark, New Jersey, for shipment to Europe and then fly new P47s from Farmingdale on Long Island, New York, to Long Beach for service in the South Pacific. Ferrying was a fun break from base operations.

When I returned to Aloe in the spring, I had been promoted to base operations officer. Captain Dockstaeder had been transferred shortly before my return.

Surprisingly, a captain had been made assistant operations officer; I was still a lieutenant. How this came about I never learned, but what I did learn was that my assistant, putting it kindly, was a peculiar person. I won't attempt to explain, but one thing stood out: He didn't like to fly! Many military pilots flew only when they had to fly. I never understood this because I flew every chance I got. To me, nothing was more enjoyable.

As operations officer I took advantage of the opportunity to fly several different kinds of planes that landed at our field. Some were twin-engine. At Aloe we had only T6s. I would read the tech orders on each transient aircraft before flying it. It just didn't seem right to be limited to flying single-engine airplanes.

Anyway, I overdid it. One day my superior officer ordered me not to fly visiting officers' planes. It was a sensible order. The colonel may have saved me from crashing an aircraft with which I had little familiarity and no flight instructions.

Also, the orders that transferred me to Aloe Field and denied me a chance at combat may be why I am able to write these words. Several thousand airmen were killed in the European and South Pacific Theaters. The orders I had wanted while at Matagorda, to fly overseas, could very well have made me one of the casualties. Being denied the opportunity for combat was deeply disappointing, but in retrospect I expect the denial was a blessing. Life takes strange turns.

A SEDUCTIVE OFFER

In February 1945, neither new P51s nor P47s were capable of non-stop flights across the U.S. The flight range for each of these new aircraft was so short that flights cross-country required two or three landings for refueling. There was also a flying limitation imposed on the ferry pilots by an AAF rule that prohibited any plane to be in the air after sundown. A lousy rule, but I adhered to it.

On my first trip east from Long Beach, California, my day ended in Little Rock, Arkansas. Lieutenant John Thomas, also in the Ferry Command, landed about the time I did so we went together into the city for dinner. Afterwards we took a city bus back to the air base. The bus was crowded so that Thomas and I could not sit side by side. I sat next to a pretty young woman and Thomas sat directly behind us.

The young woman and I engaged in a pleasant chat, and soon she suggested that when we left the bus I accompany her to her place. She promised me an interesting evening, making it plain that her bed would be more enjoyable than the one at the bachelor officers' quarters where I was headed.

I told her, "No thanks. I have to leave Little Rock early in the morning." I was sure that hurt her feelings because no doubt she was simply trying to do her bit for the war effort.

While Thomas and I were walking from the bus stop to the barracks, he said, "I think you should know that I heard every word you and the girl said, and Frank, you did the right thing not going home with her."

The next morning I was shaving when Thomas came into the latrine. He walked up and without so much as "Good morning," he blurted, "Say, after I went to bed last night, I got to thinking about that beautiful girl on the bus." He paused, put his face next to mine and exclaimed, "Donaldson, you're a damn fool!"

Maybe not. A year later I left active duty and came home without any crud or having been mugged.

BARREL ROLLS OVER THE PANHANDLE

My mind periodically goes back more than six decades, remembering a couple of barrel rolls over the Texas Panhandle on Tuesday, August 14, 1945.

I may also have done a loop or two as well as roll the plane. I'm sure that I hoped a Texas cowboy would see that a goofy pilot was stunting his plane "in the middle of nowhere" under a clear blue sky. No doubt the cowboy would have wondered "how come." If he thought about it later, perhaps it would have dawned on him that the military pilot had learned the war was over and that the flier was expressing his delight.

I was flying a T6 from Denver to Aloe Field at Victoria, Texas, where I was stationed when the radio came on with the announcement that the Japanese had surrendered unconditionally. World War II had ended.

As I flew back to base, the radio news went to Manhattan from where the celebration was broadcast. Scads of people in Times Square were expressing great joy; none were happier than I was.

May the Lord forgive me if I did not look up to Heaven during that flight and thank God for our nation's victory, for my own protection, and that of my sister and two brothers. I surely believe that happened; I sincerely hope so.

The war's end also meant big decision time for me. I liked the U.S. Army Air Forces, loved to fly, and would have enjoyed continuing to do so. But should I seek to remain in the service for that reason? Should I return to Birmingham, be a civilian again, perhaps not fly anymore? I had a year left in college in order to get a degree. Could I get it and remain in the service? Furthermore, Mama, a widow, was in Birmingham alone; all four of her children were away: Andrew in the Navy (submarine duty), Bernice a Spar (women's branch of the Coast Guard Reserves), and David in the Merchant Marine.

During the next several weeks I weighed all these considerations and others. Even if I chose to continue in the service, that decision would not be mine alone to make; the military decides whom it wants to keep on duty. Perhaps most important: It became apparent to me that the military life was not uplifting to my morals as a single man. So my decision to leave the service might ultimately be substantially influenced by my deeply felt need to seek a strong Christian environment.

However, the decision about remaining in the Army Air Forces or returning to Birmingham came as one of the few truly inspired moments in my life. I relate some of the details separately in the next story "Words From Above."

So I was discharged from active duty in the Army Air Forces January 19, 1946, as a captain.

WORDS FROM ABOVE

In December 1943, I became engaged to a lovely 21-year-old native Texan living in Arkansas City, near Strother Field, Kansas, where I was a pilot instructor. No wedding date was set, nor would it ever be.

The bare fact, about which I've never had any doubt, is that her parents loved me more than she did. We became warm friends and remained so for the remainder of their lives.

The girl's father was a Presbyterian minister who had accepted church pastorates in several cities, which accounted for the family residing in Arkansas City.

Following my transfer from Strother to Aloe Field, Texas in May 1944, the engagement flew downwind. On a date in 1945 that I can't nail down, the young lady to whom I was engaged made it plain that the engagement was hopeless and over with. For me to say that I was upset is putting it mildly. But I recovered quickly; an unbelievably wonderful experience at Aloe Field helped me overcome my disappointment. I probably hold the world record for the shortest time a lover nursed a broken heart.

No, not another woman! It happened as follows: One evening at Aloe my duties as base operations officer kept me near the flight line until after dark. As I left my office I walked across an open field en route to the bachelor officer's quarters. The night was cloudless and a jillion stars inspired the quiet sky. While I looked at the heavens I received a clear communication: When the war ends, go back to Alabama. Return to Birmingham. What has just happened in your life, being spurned by the young lady, is itself a blessing. You will have your reward.

I felt as though a voice had spoken to me. No, I didn't hear a voice, but the messages were as plain as if the Lord had uttered the words audibly. I had a brief exhilarating sensation that I was lifted off the ground — suspended just above it.

Then I walked on. Nothing like it had I ever known. I never considered the event an epiphany, but it must have been ever so close. A glorious experience had covered my head with a Balm of Gilead. Moreover, the instruction was one I needed in order to answer a question I was pondering: Shall I become a civilian again?

A short while later, not long before I was mustered out of service, I flew from Montgomery's Gunter Field to Birmingham,

Alabama. Gunter was socked in with extremely inclement weather, but a few minutes south of Birmingham the clouds broke and the ground became visible. I looked down somewhere in Shelby County, not far from U.S. Highway 31, and asked myself "Is it possible that in one of the farm houses I see below lives a beautiful girl who will enter my life?"

A year later Patti and I met. Four years after that flight we were married.

Patti Mullins – age 18

She was 17 when I flew over her house in Helena, 15 miles south of Birmingham. In my mind I can see her as she was then, a gorgeous high school senior standing in the front yard of the family home. Although I was a mile above her, I like to believe she glanced skyward and saw me.

REMEMBERING GENERAL HAP

On November 5, 1993, Patti and I joined 23 of my WWII aviation cadet classmates at the U.S. Air Force Academy, Colorado Springs, Colorado. We were there to honor Henry H. "Hap" Arnold, who had been our commanding general, U.S. Army Air Forces. We also were celebrating the 51st anniversary of our graduation as cadets.

During the war the Air Force was part of the U.S. Army, but in the summer of 1947 Congress created the United States Air Force, a separate military branch, co-equal, so-to-speak, with the Army and Navy. In 1949 General Arnold appropriately became the five-star general of the Air Force. He died in 1950.

In 1942 the Army was drastically short of pilot instructors. General Arnold believed that a select group of young men in the service could become pilot instructors in much less time than the Army Air Forces had established for its regular pilot cadet training program. Four hundred of those who volunteered were chosen for the Class of 42-X and became General Arnold's experiment at Randolph Field. We completed flight training and appropriate ground courses in about three months. Customary training had taken several months longer. We were "Hap's guinea pigs."

A large majority of our class had private pilot's licenses and thus had a bit of one-upmanship on typical cadets, many of whom had no flying experience. I had learned to fly in 1940-41, getting my license in January 1941 in Birmingham under the federal government-sponsored Civilian Pilot Training Program.

I can't recall ever hearing predictions as to how many of the 400 cadets in the class of 42-X were expected to flunk out, but on December 13, 1942, there were 239 of us who had flown successfully through the "crash course". We received our "wings" and second lieutenant bars at a ceremony in Randolph Field Chapel.

The freshly minted officers were assigned to Kelly Field in San Antonio for one month additional training, and then were sent as instructor pilots to training bases in the Gulf Coast Training Command (later, Central Flying Training Command).

It may seem a bit belated that the first General of the Air Force would have a special ceremony at the academy 43 years after his death. Of course he had much earlier received other honors. This one came about shortly after the completion and erection of an impressive statue, situated at a prominent place on the academy grounds a few steps from Arnold Hall. Why it took so many years to get the job done I don't know.

So, 51 years after "Hap's experiment" we guinea pigs assembled with others to enjoy the speeches, unveiling of the statue, and pay tribute to him.

The ceremony took place outdoors. The guests sat on cold metal chairs. A stiff November wind blew snow directly into the face of the academy's senior chaplain as he delivered the invocation. The snow swirled over Patti and me; we expected as much and were reasonably prepared.

Former Major Frank Donaldson at the dedication of the General Hap Arnold statue. Air Force Academy - November, 1993

2007 Reunion 42X class – Hap Arnold's guinea pigs.
"The Greatest Generation"
Frank is third from left, standing

RETURN TO HOWARD

Back at Howard College I got my first taste of politics, met my dream girl, and earned a B.S. degree.

MEETING PATTI

When I re-entered Howard College in January 1946 after an absence of four years, I needed five quarters of course study to earn a B.S. degree in economics. In 15 months I would wrap up college courses that had begun in September 1939 at Southern Union Junior College, Wadley, Alabama.

The early post-war period was comprised largely of busy, happy college days. I lived at home in Birmingham with Mama, directly across Fourth Avenue South from the campus. I didn't need a car but nonetheless bought a 1941 Dodge for $1200. I had purchased a 1937 Chevrolet business coupe ($550) in the summer of 1943 while a lieutenant at Strother Field, Kansas, but had sold it in 1945 while stationed at Aloe Field, Victoria, Texas. The sale had been a mistake. I should have driven the car home. It would have been more fun for dating than a beat-up old Dodge.

During the post-war 15 months at Howard I dated thirty-three coeds, one of whom would enter my life for keeps.

On the first day of the term in September 1946, I spotted a beautiful blonde on campus. We were registering for our fall quarter courses. My next-door neighbor worked in the college registrar's office, so I asked her to introduce me to the lovely young lady. She promptly did so.

Aerial photo of Howard College by Frank Donaldson - 1941

"Patti Sue, meet Frank Donaldson, student body president, who lives next door to me."

"Frank, this is Patti Sue Mullins. Patti Sue works with me in the registrar's office."

Patti's first day on campus had sealed her marital fate.

CAMPUS POLITICIAN

As we all remember, World War II began for this nation December 7, 1941. Less remembered is that I left Howard College as a student in January 1942 and did not return until January 1946, at which time I was discharged from the U.S. Army Air Forces as a captain.

Senior at Howard College - 1947

Early in the 1946 spring term the political bug bit me and I ran for president of the student body. My Lambda Chi Alpha fraternity brothers gave their expected support and I was elected, defeating Neal Shepherd. I thought a great deal of Neal, even considered voting for him.

My campaign was aggressive, strictly upbeat and run 100 percent on a positive note. Matter of fact, there were no negative allegations from either camp, but I probably won with a stunt that wouldn't work today, or if attempted would result in sanctions.

I literally papered the campus with leaflets, but not in a way one might expect. Bernie Frost, a Howard student, and I, both WWII pilots, rented a Piper Cub at the Birmingham airport, flew low over the Howard campus and dropped hundreds of letter-size leaflets urging **DONALDSON FOR PRESIDENT**.

I don't recall the time of day we performed this masterful political maneuver, but we probably tried timing it when classes changed as the 1,500 or so students walked from one building to another. The students responded as we had hoped, picking up the leaflets.

The election went my way and I served as president until my class work and exams were completed in March 1947. A good buddy, Vice President James Hall, served as president the rest of the school year. James and I were friends the remainder of his life.

There were two principal highlights of my term as president: College President Harwell (Major) Davis told me, "I hope you will come back here some day and teach." We had gotten to know each other well because of my role in student affairs. The Howard student government bought and gave to the college an organ, which was placed in Old Main's large auditorium on the second floor.

I've never been sure what prompted the statement that I someday teach at Howard but it was very satisfying to me. As president of the student body I headed up a drive to raise funds for the purchase of that electric organ. It was used in the space where college plays, recitals, and visiting speakers held forth. I understand this organ was used in its original location until Howard moved to the Homewood campus in 1957.

So, perhaps Major Davis' kind remarks to me that I might someday be a faculty member was really an expression of appreciation for my role in the acquisition of the musical instrument. If so, I don't doubt one moment he came close to rescinding his kind words following an outrageous request I made. I asked the major if he would give the student government officers authority to obtain a city permit to rope off Fourth Avenue South between Mrs. Steven's Hash House and the Pi Kappa Phi fraternity house in order for the students to have a campus wide dance one evening "on the avenue."

My word! The major leveled a verbal boom on me. The very idea that I would think of such a preposterous thing, much less mention it, was shocking. (And he had seen combat in WWI). No! Don't ever present such a foolish request again.

As you see, I don't quote him, but I express the content of his no uncertain refusal. In late 2006 or early 2007 I inquired of Mrs. Jean Kelser, the major's long time secretary, if she remembered this incident. "Do I! There was smoke in the room."

Notwithstanding my foolish request and the major's emphatic negative reaction he didn't hold it against me. "Of course not," Mrs. Kelser said. "He was one of the kindest men I ever knew."

If the president had okayed the dance, Baptist preachers from across Alabama, and some trustees of the college, would have expressed their outrage, perhaps by even marching on the campus.

It is not likely, to put it mildly, that such a request as I made for a student dance on a public street that runs through a Baptist college campus would get a green light, even today.

I've never learned what became of the organ, but eight years from the date of its installation President Davis hired me as a part-time instructor for an evening economics course. In seven more years Major Davis' successor, Dr. Leslie Wright, brought me on in the summer of 1962 as a law professor.

Then in 1986, 21 years after Howard College became Samford University, 40 years after I asked for a campus dance on Fourth Avenue South, 46 years after entering Howard as a student, I was chosen Samford University Alumnus of the Year. About the same time the university's Cumberland School of Law awarded me its first Distinguished Service Award. Neither required that I conduct a campaign. Both were surprises. They show clearly that on a university campus that does not have a mega-enrollment a graduate has a good chance for an honor.

THE ACTOR

Shortly after returning to Howard following my four year absence during WWII, I took Miss Antoinette (Toni) Sparks' writing course and cranked out a script for a one act play for which she awarded me a C grade. Of course I thought my work was better than she did. I never kept a copy. Who knows? The C may have reflected a bit of grade-flation. Could be the reason I don't have a copy is that after she graded it the thing never again saw the light of day. Just as well.

Although Miss Sparks looked with disdain upon my play she was not deterred from giving me a lead role in two productions during the 1946-47 academic year. In Trouble Shooter she cast me as J.S. Wilson, Sr. and in Death takes a Holiday as Duke Lambert. These probably mean diddle-dee to the reader.

After our two performances several of us were initiated into "full membership" in Alpha Psi Omega, National Honorary Dramatic Fraternity composed of a "group of worthy dramatic students." Well, that's what was written in the Souvenir Memoranda of our initiation. The Memoranda also exaggerated by recording that I gave "excellent performances" in each of my two roles. I didn't take issue with the quote then or now.

Notwithstanding the foregoing flattery I must admit I was pleased that the fraternity, also referring to the two plays, published that I had the distinction of having "memorized without any annoyance to the director the most speeches of any actor of the year."

It was comforting to learn Miss Sparks was not annoyed. Perhaps the play I penned took care of that or, maybe my own annoyance with her for giving me a C was enough for both of us.

I will confirm that my track record regarding teacher annoyance is a bit hazy. Alexander Braley chewed me out royally.

He really let me have it for getting a haircut. His verbiage was so strong I must have gotten a crew cut. He made his case by pointing out that an actor shouldn't even think of a haircut the day before his stage play is to open. But I had done it.

Braley said actors wear long hair, their hair covers their ears, if not, in any case covers the top of their ears and always comes over the back of a shirt collar. My barber had cropped my hair so close it didn't touch either my ears or my collar.

That was in the 1938-39 school year at Central High in Phenix City. I was a senior and Braley was one of my teachers as well as director of the school's theater production, a play in which I had a respectable role.

I liked Braley and he liked me. He was an excellent teacher, always came to class prepared, and he knew how to skillfully draw his pupils into appropriate discussions. He was fortyish, single, and I thought a bit peculiar. With my fresh haircut he probably thought the same about me. No matter, we got along fine, before and after the haircut.

I don't recall the play we did, nor any of the lines, though I do recall that I was also in another production, on stage alone, performing as a black-face comedian. I doubt there ever was a cornier presentation. If the show had been recorded I'm sure that today I would be embarrassed to listen. Not that the material was racist, raunchy or ugly in any way, but it was so silly, hardly funny (though intended to be) and juvenile. Perhaps it was planned to be juvenile since I was a high school senior. I remember that after each punch line an old guy sitting near the back of the full house laughed aloud. Thanks.

In later years, after my law practice got underway, I took to the stage again. At that time the stage was in courtrooms before juries. From time to time an observer might come to the conclusion that the jurors were annoyed in a trial — either with me or my client, or both. I'm fully aware, and always have been, that in every trial the responsibility is that of counsel to sell his side of the case (the play) to the jury.

In the theater the actor should not annoy the director and must not annoy the audience (unless intentional). In the court room counsel had better not annoy either the jury or the judge. To do it to both in the same case might indicate the lawyer ought to leave the court cases to better actors.

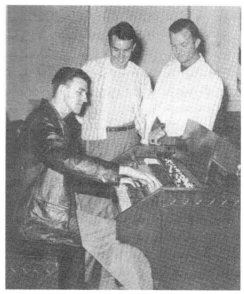

Frank Donaldson (center) with Joe McDow
(playing the organ) and William Thomas - 1947

Frank as a Senior at Howard College - 1947

| *Patti as a* | *Andrew as a* | *Nena as a* |
| *Freshman - 1947* | *Freshman - 1947* | *Freshman - 1947* |

PATTI

The dream coed says yes and
life's journey with my partner begins.

THE COURTSHIP

The first time I asked Patti Mullins to marry me she said, "No." But she said it in such a sweet, winsome way I wasn't at all discouraged.

At that time we were students at Howard College. She was a freshman and I a senior. Within a few months of my proposal we would be living in different cities for a long time.

I was graduated in the spring of 1947 and in July went to the FBI Academy in Quantico, Virginia, as a new agent.

Patti Sue Mullins
Freshman at Howard College-
1946

In October I had completed training and the bureau assigned me to Seattle for my first office. After a month in Seattle I was moved to the Spokane resident agency.

During my tour in Spokane and even after the FBI transferred me to New York City, the long-distance courtship continued.

Patti's home was in Helena, Alabama, but she lived in the women's dormitory at Howard College while she pursued her degree.

There was one stretch we did not see each other for 13 months. That was two months longer than I was away from Birmingham without a visit during WWII.

Many letters passed between us. They were fun to write, more fun to receive. Love letters are very endearing, but my opinion then and now is that long-distance romance is, as we used to say in the 20th century, "for the birds."

Patti Mullins
Engagement Photo
October 1949

We became engaged by mail. One day in the fall of December 1948, without informing her that I was going to do so, I mailed Patti an engagement ring. I had not even hinted to her what was to occur.

At the time it seemed to me the ring would send a message she could not misinterpret — that I really wanted to marry her.

Such strategy on my part was unnecessary because her letter to me saying, "Yes" to my latest written proposal and the ring passed each other in the mail.

We were engaged long distance for 10 months, not marrying until Patti was graduated from Howard in August and recovered after an appendectomy.

Well before our planned wedding in October 1949 I had selected an apartment for us in New York City, a 10th floor, one-bedroom unit in Stuyvesant Town, Manhattan — 10 minutes from my office in the Federal Building at Foley Square.

Patti never made it to New York. My work there was short-lived, which was just as well. I don't believe my bride would have enjoyed living in the big city. She had grown up in Helena, Alabama, and Helena was very small, 1,200 or fewer residents in 1949. New York City would have been frightening to her.

Fortunately I was transferred to Birmingham three weeks before our wedding.

In September 1949, Mama became seriously ill at her Birmingham home. When she was hospitalized shortly thereafter, I asked FBI Director J. Edgar Hoover for a transfer home and he promptly obliged.

I was certain that the special agent in charge of the Birmingham FBI office knew I had come to Birmingham on a hardship transfer, so I thought it well to mention to him that I soon would marry a young lady who lived nearby.

My concern was that he might think I had finagled a transfer to Alabama so my wife and I would not have to live in New York City. He said he saw no problem. "Don't give it a second thought," he said.

Twenty-one days later the long courtship ended happily. Patti and I were wed October 30, 1949, in the Helena Baptist Church.

Mama soon recovered, although she was not in good health. She lived until October 19, 1957.

Epilogue: In October 1949, because of its caseload the Birmingham FBI office needed an additional agent. As the old saw goes: "Timing is everything."

WEDDING NOSTALGIA

Snoopy of Peanuts comic strip fame would have reported, "It was a dark and stormy night." Sure, many other couples got married Saturday evening, October 30, 1949, but few in such a storm as did Patti Mullins and Frank Donaldson.

The wind blew rain horizontally across the front porch of the little Helena, Alabama, Baptist church. Umbrellas were useless; a raised one was quickly blown inside out. People who came to the wedding were soaked as they scurried from auto into the church.

Patti's mother, Ethel, understandably was fearful of ominous clouds, especially associated with thunder and lightning. She had lost her home, next door to the church, in a tornado in May 1933. The Mullins family, including then 4-year-old Patti, survived by being dumped into their basement a split second before the house was blown off its foundation and disintegrated. Eleven people in Helena were killed in the tornado, including one on each side of the Mullins' home.

At our wedding Mrs. Mullins again survived, comforted by Patti's dad, Fred, although she agonized throughout the ceremony. (Years later our daughter Susan asked whether her grandmother "agonized" over the weather or losing her daughter to a Sin City refugee.)

The Reverend James Carmichael tied the knot that has remained taut 60 years. The Rev. Carmichael had come to Helena Baptist as pastor in 1943 when worship was conducted there only every other Sunday. Three years after his arrival, members voted against a motion that he be asked to preach every Sunday, that is, to become the church's first fulltime pastor, so he promptly left for a full time pastorate in Georgia. Later that same year, the Helena church called a pastor to preach every Sunday.

(In the 1970s while writing a portion of the history of Helena Baptist, I learned that at the time of our wedding the church had been established 116 years, one of the six oldest Baptist churches in Alabama. History of the church is in the Samford University Library.)

While still a teenager, Patti had become the church's pianist and later its organist. The Rev. Carmichael and his wife Esther had become her close friends and remained so thereafter. Thus, the request for the Rev. Carmichael to conduct the marriage ceremony, notwithstanding his having lived away from Helena three and a half years.

From her childhood Patti played the piano/organ for worship, weddings, and funerals at the church. When we moved from Helena in 1978, Patti had been church pianist/organist there for 28 years. For our wedding, her friend Millie Hughes played.

My brother Andrew served as best man. Brother David was far away in the U.S. Army; sister Nena was a bridesmaid; Patti's sister Vivian (Bib) Evans was Matron of Honor. Having recently recovered sufficiently from a serious illness, Mama was able to attend.

Immediately after our stormy wedding, my bride and I drove to Montgomery. As we drove south, a cold front followed, the storm subsided and the sky cleared, so we entered the Jefferson Davis Hotel, our first stop, under a big, beautiful, golden moon.

The Jeff Davis was one of two leading Montgomery hotels. I had reserved the honeymoon suite for one night at the exorbitant rate of ten dollars!

At the time of our marriage I was a Congregationalist and Patti a Baptist. I had promised her I would become Baptist, so a couple of months after the wedding I was baptized by Dr. John Slaughter, pastor of Birmingham First Baptist Church. Patti and I became members there and attended regularly until September 1952 when we moved to Tuscaloosa and joined Calvary Baptist.

Not long ago a friend and I were reminiscing and I mentioned "the dark and stormy night" of the wedding, how it was impossible for any of us not to have gotten drenched. His apt response: "Better drenched in the wedding than soaked in the marriage!"

Frank and Patti marry at Helena Baptist Church
October 30, 1949

THE RIGHT ANSWER?

Out of the blue at breakfast one morning my wife asked, "If I die first, will you remarry?"

"That's a strange question," I responded. "You're seven years younger than I am. You know a woman's lifespan is several years longer than a man's."

"Don't change the subject," she retorted and repeated her question with obvious seriousness. "If I die first, will you remarry?"

"Listen," I said. "It's not going to happen. Your question is irrelevant."

With impatience my wife again asked her question and insisted, "Now answer me."

So I responded firmly, "No way. I wouldn't have the slightest interest in marrying again." Whereupon she began to sob. "What in the world!" I was taken aback.

"You don't love me," she exclaimed.

"But I do. You know I do."

"No, you don't. You're unhappy. I've been a failure or else you'd want another wife."

"No way is that so," I insisted, putting my arms around her and patting her on the back, consoling her as best I could.

At breakfast several months later, she asked, as if the question were brand new, "If I die first, will you remarry?"

"You bet," I answered enthusiastically. She began to sob.

"Great Scott!" I exclaimed.

"You don't love me. You can't wait for me to leave." She seemed distraught.

"Wait a minute," I chirped. "Something wrong? Are you ill? Are you about to conk out on me?"

"No, I'm all right," she said, adding, "But don't say conk out; that's not nice."

Was I perplexed? Yes. Within one year I answer the same question "No" on one occasion and "Yes" on another, and my wife of 50-plus years is upset with each response.

Do I understand? Of course not. I think to myself, "Maybe some day!"

Patti dressed for a
Teacher / Student Softball Game
1963

At Susan's wedding
June 8, 1991

THE FAMILY

A reason for being.

MAMA

My mother, Susie Appleby Donaldson, died on a Saturday afternoon a little more than a half-century ago. She was 76. I was 36.

More than five decades later I miss her. I thank God Mama gave me life, nurtured me, taught me, and disciplined me. Did she ever discipline me! Switching me with a peach tree branch was part of her daily routine. This went on until I was 6 or 7 years old. Then I never got another switching.

How grateful I am she made me

Susie Martha Donaldson
Birmingham, Alabama -
1941

a believer in discipline and at an early age. Perhaps that's why I've always considered corporal punishment, reasonably administered by parents to little children not inappropriate.

No school child could have had more encouragement from a parent than I had from Mom. When I was discouraged, she would say, "Shoulders back, head up, you can do it." And especially in the evening: "Get a good night's sleep, tomorrow is another day." When I doubted my ability with a particular task she would say, "You can do whatever you set your mind to do."

One day at lunch I reminded Patti that if Mother were alive and dining with us, we would discuss her 126 years. (Patti reminded me that her dad, Fred F. Mullins, Sr., would be 125).

My thoughts then went back to a visit Patti and I made to Ole Town in Albuquerque, New Mexico. While there I mentioned to her that my mind overflowed with thoughts of Mama, believing and feeling like I was walking where Mama had walked 80 to 90 years earlier. I

Susie Martha Appleby Donaldson
Probably 1920's

recalled as a child Mama told me that in the early 20th century she worked for the American Red Cross in Albuquerque. I visualized her as a brave young lady, "out West" in the "old days," rendering service to others, which was, one way or another, her lifelong contribution to humankind.

Her particular assignment, how long she was there, other details, including the events that took her more than halfway across the country from her home in Macon County, Alabama, passed from my memory, and I have no records.

When Mama returned to the southeast she somehow wound up in Morristown, Tennessee. How she, yet unmarried, and John Worley Donaldson, who became her husband and my father, got together in the first place, I don't recall hearing either of them relate.

I did learn they eloped to North Carolina by rail in October 1920. The bride was 39, the groom 68, and had been a widower for a year. Why North Carolina? Beats me, but the October leaves in that part of the country are magnificently beautiful. Shortly after the honeymoon they returned to Morristown. Eleven months later I came along. The following year Bernice was born.

Less than 4 years from their wedding they settled in Phenix City, about 40 miles from where Mama grew up in Macon County. Mama had inherited from her widowed dad 40 acres within the city limits of Phenix City.

Papa sold to his brother and business partner, George, his half interest in Donaldson Brothers Wholesale grocery in

Morristown. So with Papa's money and Mama's land they soon began developing the property.

Mama was a very bright lady with plenty of good common sense. From the time my youngest brother David was 10, Mama was a widow, and during World War II she saw all four of her children leave home.

Mama held up well during the war, even with all of us away. From time to time I flew a T-6 home to visit her on weekends. I wish I had her letters to me and mine to her, but most have been lost.

If she were here today, I would apologize to her for my having been such a pest, especially at ages 5 and 6, and causing her so much grief. Then I would hug her and say, "I love you." I wish I had said to her more often, "Mama, I love you."

I truly realize how important it is to say those words. "Patti, I love you." And she has never even had to switch me.

MAMA LEAVES US

Early Saturday afternoon on October 19, 1957, I left my law office in the Comer Building (now City Federal) in downtown Birmingham and began my drive home to Helena about 25 minutes away. My plans were to have lunch with my wife and our two sons, then drive to Birmingham's East End Memorial Hospital to visit my mother. She resided about five blocks from the hospital and had been admitted as a patient the day before.

After driving only a few blocks I thought that I should not then go home but should first visit Mama. I reasoned that something might come up at home that would delay my seeing her until the next day. Thus, I drove to the hospital.

I found Mama sleeping, not surprisingly, because 2 p.m. was naptime for her. A nurse was in her room. I commented that Mama looked good — relaxed, rested, and that her face was wrinkle-free. I added, "She seems 20 years younger than her 76 years."

The nurse shook her head, glanced at me, and as she looked away, said softly, "I'm sorry, but Mrs. Donaldson is leaving us." She explained that Mama had just gone into a coma from which she would not recover. She said that it was not unusual for a person near death to appear as Mama did — at peace with the world.

I was taken aback because Mama looked so good. Yet she was only a few minutes away from her last breath?

A short time later as I drove home I shed big tears. I had had Mama 36 years, for which I was and am grateful, but I missed by only a few minutes having a final conversation and a chance to say goodbye.

Living in Helena and working in downtown Birmingham had left me little opportunity for frequent visits with Mama. But amid my tears I rejoiced that from September 1955 through May 1957 I had visited her about once a week.

During those two years I had taught a class at Howard College, across the street from Mama's house. My classroom was less than a city block from her place. I had dropped by to see Mama before or after class. That ended in May as the 1957 fall term began on the new campus in Homewood, several miles from where Mama lived. Thus I missed our Tuesday evening chats. Of course, I visited Mama, but the visits weren't scheduled, nor were they as often as I would have liked.

I frequently visit Mama's grave site at Elmwood Cemetery. My thoughts go back to our days together. There is no way I could have had a more wonderful Mama. No way.

"Thank you, Lord, for giving Mama and me to one another."

ICING ON A WONDERFUL DAY

About 5 a.m. on Sunday, February 28, 1954, Patti whispered to me she believed our second child would be born soon. I promptly deposited our 2-year-old son, Steve, with next-door good friends Bill and Jane Donaldson (no kin).

Patti and I then drove with dispatch to Tuscaloosa's Druid

Grandmother Donaldson with Steven and David, Tuscaloosa, Alabama 1954

City Hospital, where David Allan Donaldson arrived just after 7 a.m.

An hour later Patti reminded me I had a Sunday school class to teach at Calvary Baptist Church. I decided to stop for breakfast at a drugstore on University Boulevard, two blocks from our apartment at Stoneleigh Court. The only person on duty at the drugstore was the elderly druggist, who on Sunday mornings doubled as cook.

I asked for an egg, bacon, toast and coffee. The druggist chatted cheerfully as he cooked. Of course, I told him of David's arrival, whereupon he announced the breakfast was on the house. I welcomed that news for two reasons: (1) I was in law school on the GI Bill and my scant savings, so a free breakfast was not an insignificant gift. My only job was to lock the doors to the Baptist student building each evening. My pay was $20 a month. (2) His delightful gesture came on top of one already wonderful morning.

At that drugstore in 1954, the breakfast would have cost less than a dollar, but that is not why I recall the gesture. I recall so well how the druggist/cook/store owner conveyed to me — by deed, expression, and words — his joy upon hearing of our son's birth. But despite my vivid recollection of the event, I can't recall my benefactor's name. Fifty-plus years since that day my memory lets me down.

But recalling that moment reinforces this point: How many people have touched my life in helpful, delightful ways, yet I can't remember many of the names. On the other hand, if I have per chance been a Good Samaritan and been forgotten I clearly understand.

True, I may have lent a helping hand to persons whose names I now can't call up. But to me that's understandable: I don't dwell on those names.

But shouldn't I have been careful to remember the name of my benefactor for his special kindness on that Sunday morning? I'll never forget that he put icing on my good day and made it even better.

DAVID AND THE BROKEN ARM

One afternoon in our backyard at Helena, Alabama, my ten-year-old son played a very painful game of Tarzan in a walnut tree.

David's stupid father was watching his boy swing on the limbs. I wasn't more than 10 feet away and looking directly at my son when he announced that he would jump from one limb to another. He jumped but, alas, his plans were not fulfilled. I dashed to him and pulled him to me, observing that when he smacked the ground his left arm was badly broken a few inches above the wrist.

We immediately drove to Children's Hospital in Birmingham. In a little while we were met there by orthopedic surgeon J. Kenda Jones, who soon had a cast on David's arm.

Having had a number of tumbles and having had a variety of patches for first one injury and then another, David knew well how to handle pain. Thus he handled the visit with the M.D. splendidly, although the arm understandably was very painful. With strong hands the doctor forcibly manipulated the broken bone back into alignment.

David had trouble sleeping that night and the trauma of the day's events took its toll.

In a few days our brave little lad was playing outdoors, but again too vigorously. He fell while skating and re-injured the arm despite wearing the cast.

Once more we went to see the doctor. Dr. Jones took the first cast off and reset the bone that had been separated in David's latest crash. This time everything worked out well and in a few months the arm was back in good shape, strong as its opposite member.

David played high school football and lettered three years in wrestling without further arm injuries.

Of course I didn't know at the time Dr. Jones was caring for David's arm that a few years later Dr. Jones' father and I would become good friends, although he was 15 to 20 years my senior.

It was 1968 and I was campaigning for the U.S. House of Representatives when J. Arthur Jones contacted me and said he wanted to help in the campaign. I wasn't turning down any assistance, and if I had been, his would not have been spurned.

My campaign resulted in a number of new friends, several of whom are friends yet. Had he lived, Mr. J. Arthur Jones would be one of those.

After the campaign we both continued active in the Republican Party. We got together periodically and discussed politics and other matters until his death a few years ago at (I think) age 84.

At this juncture I'm not sure how many months or years had passed after J. Arthur and I met before I learned that Dr. Kenda Jones was his son. J. Arthur had good reason to be proud of Kenda as an excellent orthopedic specialist. And I had good reason to appreciate both Arthur and his son.

And my son David has reason to appreciate Kenda.

FUN IN ATLANTA

The month was November, the year was 1964, the Saturday Alabama and Georgia Tech played their final football game against one another. A long-running series of games came to a close.

The beautiful autumn afternoon the two teams battled, my older son, Steve, and I were in Atlanta, site of the game. My visit was official business as faculty advisor to the Cumberland Law School moot court team. The three members of the team were there for the southeast regional competition, an annual fall event.

My law students argued Saturday morning freeing up Steve and me at noon for the remainder of the weekend.

What do a law professor and his twelve-year-old son visiting in Atlanta do on a Saturday afternoon with no previous plans, especially on this occasion?

I mentioned to Steve that Alabama/Georgia Tech were scheduled to play there with a 2 or 2:30 kickoff, but we had no tickets. That did not stop us from travelling to the stadium with a bit of optimism. Maybe, just maybe, we will come across 2 tickets, notwithstanding a strong likelihood the game was sold out.

When we arrived crowds of people were entering the west side of the stands, the Tech side, sun to the back of the fans. The game was to commence very shortly.

We were there only a few minutes and a lawyer acquaintance from Birmingham spoke with us. Did we get a pleasant surprise! During what one would ordinarily consider the greeting phase he asked if we could use a ticket. Of course, if we could come up with a second one. He then made me an offer: If we got another ticket and attended the event I would pay him for it sometime in Birmingham; if we did not get to see the teams play, I owed him nothing. Offer accepted. A glance at the ticket revealed it was not a bad location.

My son and I were standing close to an entrance gate, no doubt talking about what to do with only one ticket, but alert to possibilities, when a strong voice belonging to a well-dressed man, standing just inside the stadium confines, called out, "Young man, do you have a ticket?"

"No sir," Steve answered.

"You may use this one," and passed the gift to a delighted boy.

Though we both said thanks, neither of us could reach out to shake hands with our benefactor, for the opening in the screen that separated us was only large enough for the ticket to pass to the outside.

We promptly examined the gift and observed that the seat was high in the stands near the fifty yard line. Wow!

But what of our separation? Steve indicated no qualms about the location of his seat though he would be sitting among strangers and separated from his father, out of one another's sight for perhaps two and a half hours.

My ticket had me on about the fifteen yard line and less than halfway up in the stands. I'm sure the father was comforted with the good fortune we had that both of us were on the same side of the field. Steve didn't indicate one degree of anxiety. I don't recall any. Is that a clue there was none?

We agreed on the details of our after game rendezvous and went to our seats. Kickoff soon followed.

After the game my son and I met per our arrangements, walked some in downtown Atlanta, ate dinner and in a nearby theater saw the brand new movie, *Mary Poppins*.

The next day Steve could smile, knowing he was the only boy in our little town of Helena (population then about 1,500) who had over the weekend taken his first commercial airplane flight, sat in on law school moot court arguments, enjoyed the Mary Poppins movie, and had seen the exciting Bama/Tech game (for free) from a choice seat near the "Governor's Box."

To top it off the very accommodating individual, sitting near Steve, who had given him the ticket providing such a great view, listening to my son yell for Bama, loudly called out to those fans around him, "Didn't know I gave my ticket to a Bama fan!"

FATHER-SON TIME ON THE APPALACHIAN TRAIL

When my sons Steve and David were youngsters we enjoyed camping. Well, they said they did. I liked it because my sons and I had valuable time together: no radio, no TV, no telephone, no neighborhood kids, no clients or the usual societal interruptions.

Patti excluded herself. She always made it plain to the three of us, "You boys sleep in the woods on the ground all you care to, but drop me off in the nearest Holiday Inn." Never once did she make an overnight visit with us in the Back Country.

During their teens the boys also entered into many different activities, as teenagers are prone to do. While in college, Steve began mountain climbing and hiking long distances during summer recess. On one trip west in 1976 he walked the John Muir Trail for six weeks. Just prior to that hike I bought a golf bag and set of clubs from one of Steve's buddies so that the young man would have the finances to make the multi-week trip. My sports purchase was happily agreed to by Patti, even encouraged. Her son would have a traveling companion.

The Appalachian Trail was particularly inviting, relatively close to home and college and reasonably challenging. Sometimes he walked it alone, much to his mother's chagrin. So, one day when he invited me to hike with him on the Trail in North Carolina, and I agreed to do it, Patti was much pleased. As she saw it our elder son would not be alone should he encounter a huge black bear in deep woods.

On a real warm August morning in 1974, Steve and I set out on this special mission leaving our Helena home in my 1969 Chevy. We planned to hike about a week to 10 days. David was not with us; he was lifeguarding at a pool near home.

Steven and I made our first stop in Athens, Tennessee, and spent the night in an old downtown hotel in a small room with two very narrow beds. I shelled out $8 total. There was no parking charge; I had left our car on the street next to the curb and visible below our second floor room.

The next day we dropped by a federal ranger station and got our permit to hike and camp. We left the car near Fontana Dam, walked across the dam with our backpacks and headed north on the Appalachian Trail.

The temperature was in the 90s and to me our every step seemed uphill. My 25-pound backpack soon weighed 50 pounds.

As we walked (and I huffed), I recalled that the ranger who issued our permit had asked me, "You ready for the mountain?" I never hesitated to reveal my confidence. "Think so, I've been playing handball three to five times a week for years."

I felt like the temperature was 100°; it surely seemed so. My confidence to hike through the Smokies on that famed walking trail diminished with each step. As noted, every step was uphill.

The downside of the upgrade climb really hit home when I suggested to Steve we take a breather. "Breather" is the right word because at 6,000 feet I couldn't seem to get enough air in my lungs. I felt like I needed a dose of pure oxygen!

We sat a few minutes, cooled off a tad and walked again. Still uphill, of course. Soon I suggested we rest again, and we did.

I don't recall how many times we stopped to rest before Steve offered to carry my backpack as well as his own. The very idea, my 22-year-old son toting both packs. I wouldn't dream of letting him do such a thing, although I really did find the pack burdensome to lug. Very much so. I would have been delighted to get rid of it, not to have carried it another step, but I just couldn't let Steve do it for me.

Finally I said, "I'm cutting out." Steve was a good sport as we headed back toward square one near the dam.

I found that walking downgrade was less taxing, although it wasn't comfortable; the sun still bore down hard.

I'm sure Steve wanted to continue alone on the planned journey. However, I'm also sure he wasn't certain his father could successfully traverse our earlier route and find his car. Thus he stayed with me.

We put our gear and ourselves in the car not long before dark, and soon we had a room in a nearby motel.

During the evening a ferocious thunderstorm struck. From our window we watched ball lightening roll down the mountainside not far from us.

Of course, it occurred to me that, had I not pooped out and we had continued our hike, we would have been camping somewhere on the mountain, probably in the heart of the storm, and perhaps had ball lightening rolling over our prostrate bodies.

The next morning we turned in our permits to the ranger. I was embarrassed to confess to him that my many years of regular, vigorous handball play was not enough training for hot summer "mountain climbing" with a pack on my back.

Early that fall Coach J.T. Haywood and I were talking in front of the Samford University gym when a petite young woman, holding the hand of a 2 or 3-year-old child, asked, "Coach, do you mind if I run the stadium steps?"

He replied, "Help yourself." She volunteered that every autumn she and her husband trained for a couple of months before "we hunt goats in the mountains."

Run up and down the stadium steps? Not me! Too strenuous. I wouldn't have done it even if it had meant I would then be able to jog the Appalachian Trail.

On that torrid August day in 1974 when I gave the Trail a go, and it gave me a no-go, I was 52 years old.

Steve is 56 and as I write this he is hiking in the Rockies. Now a Samford University professor (Ph.D) with no summer classes to teach, he has opportunity to traipse in the mountains (although with five children, he is greatly restricted.)

The Appalachian Trail is a breeze for Steve. Even in August.

For me, there hasn't been another mountain hike, and won't be, even if someone carries my backpack.

DAUGHTERS: OUR SECOND FAMILY

Steve arrived in 1951, David in 1954, and for years thereafter Patti periodically mentioned that the presence of a daughter would give her much joy. Not that she didn't have joy with two bright and loving sons whom she adored. But, she couldn't put cute little dresses on them, and long hair on the boys didn't seem appropriate.

For all I knew, Patti was thinking that I might need a daughter (or two) to care for me in the years of my dotage.

September 30, 1965, from her hospital bed Patti said, "My prayers have been answered," as she held daughter Sharon. Her prayers were answered again August 11, 1967, upon Susan's birth into the family. At that time our sons were 15 and 13 and in high school. In a few months Steve would have his driver's license, and David would be on the Shades Valley High School wrestling team. David also soon would be pestering me to let him play football. (The pestering prevailed; he played on the Shades Valley football team two years and lettered three years in wrestling.)

The year Susan started to school, Sharon entered the third grade; David began his sophomore year at the University of the South, Sewanee, and Steve entered his senior year at Samford University.

With the boys living on their respective campuses, our at-home family had shrunk from six to four, giving Patti opportunity to provide full parental attention to her two answered prayers.

Frank and Patti with
Steve (left) and David (right)
Sharon (right) and Susan(left)
August 1968

There was even a stretch when I regularly told the girls bedtime stories — stories that I cooked up, many dozens of them, an original one each night. Most were corny, had similar plots, and the same characters, but my little coeds never grew tired of them, always asking for "one more."

Donaldson Family 1972

I like to think that about two of each hundred of those stories were quite good. We'll never know for sure as none were recorded.

In recent years my daughters have commented on those yarns, always with grins that carry more meaning than their father can discern.

I truly enjoyed my part in rearing the girls, although as one might expect, there were anxious moments. But the daughters and their parents were bountifully blessed.

Thinking of being blessed with those lovely girls reminds me of my brother Andrew and his four daughters. When his first one was born, he was upset because he had so badly wanted a boy. He was outspoken in his disappointment. But he got over it — did he ever!

Andrew revealed his change of heart one day as I was visiting him. As his four daughters played in the yard, he said, "See those girls," pointing to them as they joyfully flitted about in front of their home. "I'd rather have any one of them than 10 boys."

My unspoken response: I have the best deal in town — two and two.

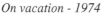

On vacation - 1974   *At home - 1974*

TEMPORARY TEXANS

Each of our two daughters was graduated from Samford University; Sharon twice, getting her B.A. in 1987 and a J.D. in 1990 from the Cumberland School of Law.

Susan was awarded her B.A. in 1989 and spent the next two years at Texas Woman's University, Denton, Texas, where she earned a master's degree in occupational therapy.

Sharon, having joined a Dallas law firm shortly after passing the Texas bar exam in July, 1990, and Susan being in graduate school meant that Patti and I had two temporary Texans in the family.

Sharon was in Texas for about a year and Susan for two years. Both returned to Birmingham, Sharon to clerk for a federal judge and later to practice law, and Susan to work for a hospital in the therapy field.

With our daughters in Texas, Patti and I made several auto trips there from Birmingham, 12 hours each way to Dallas, even longer to Denton. These very, very time consuming journeys were mostly along interstates with no personality. Nonetheless, being with our daughters made them fun visits.

After our daughters returned to Birmingham, married and had children, Patti and I (Patti much more) found that we had exchanged the 12-hour travel time to Dallas for baby-sitting time.

In the years since our grandchildren arrived, our baby-sitting hours have been sufficiently long to have driven to Texas and returned to Birmingham many times. As for baby-sitting, obviously it can be very, very time-consuming.

So what, we'll baby-sit! Let others drive to Dallas.

Still in love - 1997

TOGETHERNESS

I've lived to become an extremely wealthy man, for no value can be placed upon the invaluable—the priceless family ties that bind.

FIFTY YEARS...TWO HOUSES AND ONE WIFE

Patti and I married in October 1949, and we paid a bundle in rent before we moved into our first house in May 1958.

I doubt that today there are very many lawyers in these parts who practice law three and a half years before buying a house. That occurred with me, for I had begun my law practice October 1, 1954. (When I married I was an FBI agent; later I would enter law school.)

Patti, our sons Steve and David, and I had resided in Helena, Alabama before we built our new and first house. To say that we "built" it is not literally accurate. William Bell, a neighbor and longtime brick mason, decided he would like to try his hand at home construction, so I entered into a "lock-and-key" contract with him for a one-story residence on Rolling Mill Street in Helena.

The house would be three blocks from the post office, two blocks from Mullins Grocery and Helena Baptist Church, and four blocks from the L & N passenger train depot and the Helena School, grades one through nine.

Imagine a 1,200-square foot house, plus a carport and storage room for $10,500, contract price.

Helena, Alabama Donaldson house
February 1960

Fred Mullins, Patti's father, had recently sold us the lot next door to his and Patti's mother's house for $300, approximately one-half the value at the time.

Our contractor, Mr. Bell, was a top-notch brick mason. No one could build a better fireplace, which we had him place in the living room.

For several reasons we opted for the exterior of the house to be green cedar shake. Too bad, as Mr. Bell's masonry would have been superior quality.

Since 1952 Helena had owned its water system. The water flowed abundantly from what the locals called an artesian well, 405 feet deep. However, the town operated no sewage disposal system. Therefore we had a septic tank installed, with appropriate field lines for the bathroom. We also installed a grease-trap for the kitchen with a separate field line.

When we moved to Helena in 1955, no Birmingham lending institution, (fewer than 20 miles away), would make a home loan in Helena; it was said to be too far out in the boondocks. Helena's population then was 1,200 with dim prospects for an increase. Today's population exceeds 16,000.

There was no fire protection, and that worked against our obtaining a loan. Law enforcement was minimal: a part-time police officer, plus the sheriff's office 30 minutes away. Helena residents were little concerned by the paucity of law officers; after all, crime was practically nil.

After acquiring the Helena lot in early 1958, I looked about for home financing. The president of the bank in Columbiana

Patti and Frank, April 1984

143

asked, "You have a checking or savings account with us?"

"No," I replied.

"The bank makes loans only to its depositors."

I departed. I had not the slightest interest in establishing a bank account in Columbiana. My residence was in Helena and my law office was in Birmingham. Columbiana was a 30-minute drive in the wrong direction.

Believing in the potential for housing in the boonies, a Birmingham company was expanding its home mortgage business, so I landed a mortgage with that company: a $9,800 loan at 6% interest, payable $78 a month including taxes and interest for 20 years.

While living in our little house, Patti and I added two daughters: Sharon in 1965 and Susan two years later.

Until Steve left home in 1970 to attend Samford University and David in 1972 for the University of the South, our little abode was crowded.

Oh yes, Ethel Lovelady Mullins, Patti's mother, lived with us from the day her husband, Fred, died on September 29, 1971 until she passed away on March 10, 1982.

The girls, Mrs. Mullins, Patti and I were in the Helena "home place" until we moved into our new Homewood quarters in September 1978.

My 23 plus years commuting from Helena to Birmingham had finally ended. I had swapped a 25 to 30-minute commute for a four minute one. Joy!

I write this home-ownership record while sitting in my study at 107 Lucerne Boulevard, Homewood, Alabama. We built this house under a lock-and-key contract at a cost approximately eight times that of the Helena place. Here we have 3,600 square feet of living space, plus a deck, front porch, screened back porch, carport and storage room.

Only Patti and I are here. Our daughters left in the 1990s for their own homes and families. The sons had gone on their own in the 1970s. So, Patti and I have a place with five bedrooms, three baths, living room, den, study, playroom, dining room, kitchen, and laundry room.

Homewood, Alabama house and doggie, Daisy 1990

The irony: At one time the six of us and Mrs. Mullins lived in Helena in a house with 1,200 square feet and one bathroom. Today two of us live in three times the space. Nostalgia creeps into my soul when I think of that. Frankly, I'll take the small house with Patti and all the kids! Perhaps I shouldn't say it; it's just that I loved the years when the kids were growing up and all sleeping under the same roof.

Occasionally our 11 grandchildren and their parents visit us. That makes 21 of us, and guess what happens? Our expansive home begins to shrink and for a delicious while it's comfortably small again. And indescribably cozy. The way it used to be.

CHOICES

After being graduated from the University of Alabama law school in 1954, I returned to Birmingham with Patti and our two sons.

William A. Thompson and I opened a law office in the Comer building (now City Federal), downtown, on Second Avenue North. We practiced in a 50/50 partnership for seven years before I moved into a solo practice in the Frank Nelson Building, one block west on 20th Street.

In my early years in law practice I was in the Air Force Reserve and served on active duty one evening a month and pulled a 15-day tour of duty in each of three years, 1955, 1956 and 1957. The last two years of reserve duty were with the Judge Advocate General's Corps in the Air Force. Upon Patti's request I had switched from flight status in late 1955. I would have preferred to continue flying but Patti observed sensibly that as I grew older my reflexes would become slower — as the fighter planes got faster —and that just didn't add up the way it should.

Sometime in late 1957 I gave up the active reserve altogether as it required too much time. This meant abandoning 10-plus years in the reserve (and I had had nearly four years active duty service during WWII). And it also meant the foregoing of a reserve retirement check beginning at age 60. No regrets. None. My family deserved more of me — and I of them.

I gave up regular Saturday golf so that the boys, Patti and I could have quality time together. Patti was pleased. Frankly I never looked upon my golf exodus as a sacrifice. My sons, and later my daughters, were paramount, great fun and unbelievably wonderful gifts to Patti and me.

Golf is fun and frustration, and can be great exercise if one walks, doesn't ride, and plays frequently. Nevertheless golf sucks up one's time like a vacuum cleaner sucks up dust. Even so, I returned to the game in a big way when my daughters graduated from Samford University and left home. Circumstances often dictate one's choices.

EATING OUT

We are an eating-out society. Just try finding a good restaurant Friday evening without a long wait before being seated.

Oh, making reservations doesn't get a person to the head of the line. Not all good eating places in the part of the world where I live will reserve tables. Besides, reservations can tie one to an undesirable schedule. So, reservations just don't appeal to me.

It's not just Friday evenings that dining out is popular; other nights the restaurant business is booming. Sometimes there is a wait at breakfast time — even a long line of customers at fast-food places.

Of course, it hasn't always been that way.

A recent morning during our breakfast at home, I mentioned to Patti an article in The Birmingham News that reported government welfare rolls were shrinking, and that as a result charities needed more money to feed hungry people.

Patti commented that during the Great Depression her family (Mom and Dad and three children) had very little food, got no handouts or welfare of any sort, ate sparingly at every meal, and always ate at home. "Except," she said, "I remember one time Daddy took us all to lunch at the Empire Steak House in Birmingham. He ordered oysters; where he got the money I have no idea."

Well, I have an idea. Fred Mullins had sold a cow. Patti's dad (one of my heroes and a dear friend) had a few cattle on his then-mortgaged farm. Once in a while he hauled one of them to a Birmingham stockyard next to the First Avenue viaduct and got a few dollars, which he spent for necessities.

No doubt the oysters were a splurge of the most reckless kind for Fred. Patti's mother, Ethel, probably had a hissy fit about such wild spending. Total cost for the family meal that day probably was less than three dollars.

In those tough depression era days a café hamburger cost a dime and an RC Cola a nickel. At the grocery store a loaf of sliced bread was also a nickel; a gallon of buttermilk bought at a farmer's door was 10 cents.

Even so, there were many hungry people. Surely they had no money to eat at a café. Even people who did have a little cash didn't dine out very often. The café operators worked long hours but not many could expect to retire young.

A man getting a bit of food from a "bread line" often took it to his family, although he was likely to nibble on it on the way home.

During my boyhood days in Phenix City, which included lean pocketbook years, my family never ate out. Never, ever. From the time we moved to Phenix City from Morristown, Tennessee (I was almost 3), every meal we had was consumed at home. This was not because my father did not have the money; he could have taken Mama and us kids to a restaurant now and then, perhaps even across the Chattahoochee River to Columbus, Georgia, but Papa seldom spent a dime he didn't have to spend. He squeezed every penny till Lincoln hollered, as we say.

His thriftiness never rubbed off on me, though many of my ancestors lived in Scotland. The Scottish blood just never got in my veins.

As a boy I took my lunch sandwiches to school every day from the first grade through 12th. I never once purchased a school lunch. I also brought milk from home. The women who operated the lunchroom allowed me to keep my milk in the school's refrigerator.

I finally ate in a school lunchroom when I entered college and was living away from home.

THE HARVEST

My father had told me that not long before he and my mother married in 1920 that he planted several apple trees on his Morristown, Tennessee, property. He was 67 or 68 years old at the time. While he was planting, a neighbor asked, "Old man, why are you putting out those apple trees? You won't live to eat any apples from them."

Papa said he replied, "So what, if I never see an apple, it doesn't matter. I have children and grandchildren who will enjoy the fruits from my labor."

Those trees put forth lots of apples during my father's lifetime, which brings me to the following (nutty) true stories.

Son David's two horses ate the bark from half the 20 pecan trees I planted in 1962 on the two acres just behind our house in Helena. The loss of those Stuarts and Mahans left me with only 10 trees of the same varieties. How those thriving trees survived the animal's teeth I don't know, but by the time Patti and I and our two daughters moved to Homewood in September 1978, the trees were beginning to produce pecans (albeit a small crop compared to the quantity I gathered 25 years after they were planted.)

We sold the two acres in 1996 without retaining right of ingress, thus releasing all the pecans to the property purchaser. Several houses were built among the trees and the place was named "The Pecan Grove."

At the time we moved to Homewood I noticed that our lot was big enough for at least one pecan tree. We had removed eight to ten large pine trees from the property, leaving room for both the house and one or more trees. But Patti vetoed a pecan tree because, she said, squirrels would prevent our getting any nuts and I would waste time and energy planting a tree for benefit of the squirrels, which were bountiful in 1978.

I was disappointed but acquiesced. I was 56 and aware that 15 to 20 years would elapse before a tree would produce lots of nuts. Nonetheless, I thought, "So what if I never see a pecan, that doesn't matter; our children and grandchildren will enjoy the nuts from my labor."

A few days ago as I walked in my neighborhood I noticed a squirrel carrying a nut, and the matter of the pecans struck me afresh. Why not plant a pecan tree, perhaps a pecan nut, and hope to see it sprout and grow? After all, my fondness for pecans goes back to my boyhood.

In our yard in Phenix City there were four pecan trees, all grown from nuts planted by my mother when she was young. The largest was beautifully shaped and provided enjoyable shade in hot months. The tree grew near the family well, and that meant plentiful water for it even in dry spells. I will always believe the big tree's roots tapped into our home water supply. No wonder it outgrew the other trees.

More important than size, the big pecan tree was a fabulous producer of large soft-shell nuts.

Starting when I was a small boy and on through my teen years, I enjoyed climbing that superb tree every October, shaking the limbs, reaching the outer branches with a cane pole and slapping down pecans by the basket.

I'm certain that 25 years and more after Mama had planted those nuts she delighted in the annual harvest of pecans.

So, Mama had her pecans and Papa had his apples, but their son, to have either, must visit the market. However, plenty of acorns fall in my yard from a neighbor's tree and there are squirrels galore.

A TRUE FRIEND

Fred F. Mullins, 39 years my senior and father of my wife, once said to me, "I'd rather have friends than money. If I have friends I can get money." At the time, these words were put in the proper context, although my wife and I occasionally have pondered the full meaning of the last part of the comment.

When I first met "Mr. Fred" in 1946 while courting his daughter, I could not anticipate that nine years later Patti and I, with our two sons, would move into his and his wife Ethel's home, and that my father-in-law would become my most generous friend, ever. No, I never borrowed a penny, but my family and I lived in his home without charge during the time I had insufficient funds for housing.

Upon my graduation from the University of Alabama law school in August 1954, William A. "Bill" Thompson and I opened a partnership law office in Birmingham's Comer

Fred and Ethel Mullins with grandsons Steve and David, Helena, Alabama - 1961

Building (now City Federal). At that time Patti and I and our sons Steve and David, moved in with Mama in Birmingham. (We stored our furniture). We were with Mama about four months, then we rented a small house in east Birmingham.

During the winter of 1954 David became seriously ill with bronchitis. It happened when my attorney fees were slim pickings. So in May 1955, with our rent paid but having no money to pay more, coupled with our need to get David out of Birmingham's pollution, we moved into the Mullins home in Helena.

Patti and I helped buy groceries; Patti prepared meals and kept house (she is a really good cook and housekeeper!).

On October 19, 1957, Mama died at age 76 in a Birmingham hospital. She had been a widow 19 years and her income (no Social Security) was from several rental houses in Phenix City, Alabama. With her good management and frugal living, the rental income had adequately sustained her.

After Mama's death, I sold all her Phenix City property as well as her Birmingham home and divided the proceeds equally among her four children.

Although my law practice income had reached the point of sustaining my family, Patti and I used our portion of the inheritance to help us build a house in Helena next door to her parents on a lot Mr. Fred sold us for a nominal sum.

We moved into our new home in May 1958, and lived there 20 years and three months. David's bronchitis promptly disappeared after our arrival in Helena, a testimony to clean air.

For 23 years I commuted to work in Birmingham, averaging about 25 minutes travel time each way.

As the years went by I did legal work for Mr. Fred, qualifying him for Social Security, handling his real estate transactions and other matters. Patti spent many hours and days caring for both Mr. Fred and Miss Ethel in their last years.

No amount of pro bono legal work or other favors I could have performed would have repaid Mr. Fred for his willing generosity extended to my family and me during our time of near penury.

Mr. Fred and Miss Ethel enabled me to continue in private law practice that led directly to the invitation I received to become a law professor, a position that developed into the crowning jewel of my legal career. Indeed, "I'd rather have friends than money."

"DEAR DADDY" FROM A DEAR ONE

12-14-99

Dear Daddy,

Merry Christmas! I decided this would be a good time to share with my favorite Dad just how wonderful I think he really is. Thinking back on my childhood I can come up with some specific memories of you and some of the things we did together.

One of my favorites is of you taking us to the pool at Samford practically every Saturday afternoon in the summer so we could swim. I don't remember you having anything else to do on those days although I'm sure you did. All I know is that Sharon and I looked forward to those outings just as I looked forward to our afternoon walks and explorations with the family dog. These were always activities that were just Dad and the girls. What fun and what memories you created!

Another thing I'm glad you did for me (us) is take us on all those family vacations. I know it wasn't easy on you or Mom to travel all over the country with us when we were little, but I have great memories of most of the places we visited. It created a desire in me to see more of the world and experience unusual and exciting activities.

I also remember you playing ball with us and hide- and- seek, (especially the time I busted my nose on the kitchen doorframe when I slid across the freshly waxed floor).

Dad, I guess what I am trying to say is that you are a number-one Daddy. You listened when I ranted or cried about one thing or the other, usually boys. And then said your classic line, "Sweetie, you're just fatigued. Things will look better in the morning." It wasn't always true and sometimes it made me mad, but you were right on many occasions!

I also want to thank you for trying to warn me about boys, especially about what walking bags of hormones teenage and college-age boys can be. You probably thought I wasn't listening since I usually said, "Oh Daddy, he's not like that." But I do remember all those talks and especially now that I have daughters of my own I appreciate them even more. Now I wish I had taken notes!

Thanks for always taking time with me; to talk on the phone, take walks, let me do your filing at the law school even though I didn't do such a great job, and play games.

You've always challenged me to do my best, sit up straight and not settle for mediocrity. However, I don't ever remember you criticizing me, and I don't think many kids could say that about their Dads.

Thanks for loving me unconditionally, I could go on but I'm starting to cry and I don't want to short-circuit the computer.

I love you, Dad, because you are the best Daddy in the whole world.

Always your baby,

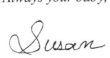

A HITCH IN THE FBI

In five years the FBI transferred me from the East Coast to the West Coast to the East Coast to the Deep South, but after marrying I was not transferred. So, who said Director Hoover frowned on marriage?

THE BUREAU'S NEW AGENT

In the spring of 1947 I heard that the FBI was hiring college graduates who had neither a law nor accounting degree. Standing policy had been new agents had to have one or the other. Many agents had resigned at the end of World War II, which caused a serious shortage of investigators. (During WWII agents had draft deferments.)

Frank in Washington 1948

I had neither degree, only a BS in economics, but with the temporary change in the bureau's employment policy and because I was 25, the minimum age qualification, my interest in becoming an agent had perked up.

I had been sorely disappointed during WWII in not being permitted to serve overseas as a fighter pilot in the U.S. Army Air Forces. So the prospect of excitement as an FBI agent, the opportunity to work in different cities on challenging assignments resulted in my willingness to engage in oral and written interviews, and to undergo the medical exam. Finally, a letter of appointment arrived from FBI Director J. Edgar Hoover.

I was sworn in as an agent July 25, 1947, and spent most of the next 10 weeks at the FBI Academy at Quantico, Virginia, attending school for new agents. A small part of our instruction was in the Department of Justice Building in Washington, D.C.

FBI Academy – Quantico, Virginia
1947

At the conclusion of our training we received our first office assignments. Mine was Seattle.

Another new agent, John DiMarchi of Hibbing, Minnesota, who had become a good friend of mine at the academy, was assigned to Birmingham and that greatly displeased him. "I think I will quit and go home," he told me.

"No, John," I argued. "Give Birmingham a try. If you don't like the place, then quit." Whether or not my advice influenced him, John went to Birmingham and served his tour of duty in Alabama, as I did in the state of Washington. Later both of us were transferred to New York City. We communicated periodically, although we were not on the same squad.

After a few months in New York, John said to me, "See this arm (holding up his full right arm), I'd give this to be back in Birmingham, Alabama."

Four Birmingham FBI Agents – 1951
Agent Donaldson, far right

All but two months of my Seattle assignment were in the Spokane resident agency; the shorter stint was in Seattle. I liked living and working in Spokane (actually I've liked every place I've lived, including New York City). For years I've said that, next to Birmingham, Spokane is my favorite city. I worked long, hard hours there. There were three reasons: the work was interesting, there was plenty of it and I was not married, which meant zero home responsibility.

In that approximate year of labor I probably aged five years. My father once said, "Hard work never killed anybody." True or not, I learned from experience that long work days (and sometimes nights) with heavy responsibilities can speed up the aging process.

This was also made plain to me by my brother Andrew's blunt remark. After being away for 13 months, I came home on leave. Andrew met me at the Birmingham Airport and his first words were, "You sure have gotten old." I was 26.

I had a short tour of duty in the Washington, D.C. field office and was transferred to New York City. Another agent and I obtained a room at the home of an elderly widow in Brooklyn. She owned the premises, a row house. I think the address was 540 16th Street. In any event the residence was only a short distance from Prospect Park, just a 20-minute subway commute to the FBI office in the federal building at Foley Square. Not bad. The fare was 10 cents each way.

I parked my 1947 Studebaker on the street in front of the widow's residence and usually moved it only on Saturday, most often to drive to a golf course, sometimes to Bethpage on Long Island. The Bethpage courses were not far from the Republic aircraft plant where I had picked up new P-47s when I was on temporary duty with the Ferry Command during WWII.

In September 1949, Mama became seriously ill, then hospitalized in Birmingham. I asked FBI Director J. Edgar Hoover for a transfer. He promptly approved it. I probably would have resigned had he denied the request.

In 1950, I wrote to Mr. Hoover, informing him that Mama had recovered, that I was in position to be transferred, although I preferred to remain in Birmingham. I never heard from him until I departed the FBI in June 1952. At that time Mr. Hoover formally accepted my resignation.

Never once have I regretted leaving the FBI. Resigning was a good decision just as joining the FBI had been a good decision. Occasionally I have asked myself, "What did that five-year hitch in the FBI mean to me?"

The answer has been easy:

- Fellow agents were top-quality and good friends.
- Many cases always were pending, thus I gained much experience. One month in Spokane I had a role in 80 cases.
- A variety of fascinating and challenging cases always were underway, so there was substantial personal satisfaction while I rendered needed public service.

- Director Hoover was a hard taskmaster who expected good work and much overtime, but he was always fair.

- Pride. I was fortunate to have been an agent in a well-run government entity, especially during the years when both the director and the FBI were respected, even admired, nationally and respected worldwide.

Fifty-plus years have passed since I left the bureau, and my fondness continues. I've long been active in the Birmingham ex-agents chapter.

My service in the FBI also meant that nearly 30 years after I left the agency, President Reagan in early 1981 looked favorably upon my FBI service in naming me to be U.S. Attorney for the Northern District of Alabama.

Epilogue: I was told my old friend, John DiMarchi, who would have given an arm to remain in Birmingham, made a career in the FBI, never leaving New York City.

THE DISPOSSESSED

One day (a long day!) in early 1948, while working for the FBI in Spokane, Washington, I solved a bank robbery.

A branch bank in Spokane was held up by a robber the teller said, "Might be a woman." The person was dressed in such a way the teller could not make a positive male or female identification.

I interviewed people at and near the holdup scene. One of those contacted was a salesman who sold paint in a single-story building on the corner of the block about three similar buildings from the bank. He told me that at about the time of the robbery a taxi parked on the street beside the store around the corner from the bank. He said a woman got out and walked in front of the paint store toward the bank. A man sat on the back seat of the cab.

A few minutes had passed he said, when the woman returned and the cab left.

I checked with the cab company and found the driver, who said he drove from the address near the bank to a downtown movie theater where the man got out. The cabbie said he then took the woman to a house he pointed out to me.

The taxi driver described the woman as the teller had: head wrapped with a scarf, no hair visible and no make-up, but the cabbie added that the person was a quite masculine-looking female.

A search warrant was obtained. Another agent and a Spokane city detective and I went to the house identified by the taxi driver. A woman and her 5-year-old daughter were present. The woman (white, heavy build, short hair) promptly confessed to the robbery. She said her husband took the bank's money while in the cab and had not returned home.

An address book found at the residence carried the names and addresses of several relatives, one of whom was a brother of the man involved. The woman volunteered that the brother's home in Memphis, Tennessee, was the most likely place her husband would be found.

A Teletype with details of events was sent immediately to the Memphis FBI office and advised an arrest warrant had been issued for the male subject. The next morning the Spokane subject and a Memphis agent arrived at the same time at the address set out in the Teletype. The agent made an easy, quick arrest.

A few weeks later the two defendants pleaded guilty, and were sentenced by a federal judge, the woman to five years and her husband to six, although he had never entered the bank.

I had worked all day and all night on the case and was elated with the good results. However, there was a downside to it all. Neither the FBI nor the U.S. Attorney (then or now) had facilities for the care and maintenance of a 5-year-old. Fortunately in this case the city detective who had been with us at the suspects' house at the time of the woman's arrest took the child to the appropriate state agency. The successful investigation and the convictions, resulting in prison time for both defendants, meant that I had played a prominent role in making a small child homeless.

So the real downside is that a 5-year-old losing both parents became an orphan. In any event she became a ward of the state. The thought struck me that this dispossessed child might never again see her parents.

It is recorded in Numbers 14:18: "The iniquity of the fathers is visited upon the children…"

But suppose the robbery had never been solved. Would the child have been better off growing up with bank robbers? Would the sins of the parents nonetheless have been "visited" upon the child?

Frank and Patti with William Webster, Director of the FBI
October 1981

Frank in the FBI - 1951

PROFESSOR DONALDSON

*The only curse of this law professor's academic life
is grading papers.*

TEACHER: BE GOOD TO YOUR STUDENTS

In the spring of 1962 I was enjoying my law practice in
downtown Birmingham when Dean Arthur A. Weeks approached
me and asked if I might be interested in joining the Cumberland
Law School faculty for the 1962-63 school year.

I later learned that this inquiry by the dean resulted from a
suggestion by Harold P. Knight, Birmingham attorney and
longtime personal friend. Harold knew that I had had an interest in
college-level teaching, for he and I each had taught in the Howard
College evening program for several semesters. Harold continued
to teach for many years.

My response about joining the law faculty was, "I'd like to
give it a whirl." There was no question about my continuing full-
time law practice because during the academic year the law school

and I would "size up" each other. I thus had an unusually busy nine months as lawyer and professor.

The Cumberland School of Law situated in Lebanon, Tennessee, since the 1840s had been acquired by Howard College in 1961. (Howard became Samford University in 1965.)

At the time Howard purchased Cumberland, Arthur Weeks was practicing law in Birmingham. Arthur had had a substantial role in Howard's acquisition of the law school. No doubt this stemmed from his having served as Cumberland Dean at Lebanon 1947-1954. He had promptly accepted the offer to be dean of Howard's new law school.

Near the end of the 1962-63 academic year, I decided that teaching law was so appealing that when Dean Weeks and Howard President Leslie Wright invited me to join the law school on a permanent basis, I happily accepted. Upon my inquiring about practicing law part-time, the president said, "Part-time, yes, with the understanding the law school is your No. 1 client." I agreed.

In a few years I was promoted from assistant professor to associate professor and to associate dean, then not long afterwards to full professor with tenure.

In early 1971, I begged to be relieved of administrative duties, but upon request of the university administration, held off a year before relinquishing these duties. (I haven't had any formal administrative responsibilities in the law school since 1973.)

Dean Weeks left Cumberland in October 1972, moving to Wilmington, Delaware, to become dean of the Delaware Law School, in my view a very wise move.

Don Corley, who only three years earlier had been one of my law students and then in his second year on the faculty an assistant professor, was named acting dean of our fast-growing law school. He didn't know diddlee-dee from diddlee-dum about the important day-to-day duties of a law school dean. But he soon was named the dean (not acting). Because Don had excellent skills in his sharp brain, and with the splendid cooperation of the faculty he succeeded in becoming an outstanding administrator. Unfortunately, cancer would take him from this life after a deanship of 12 years.

A number of people asked: How could a new assistant professor, 14 months on the job, be made acting dean? The answer is easy: Samford University President Leslie Wright wanted a dean he could dictate to without any static, as in: "Here's the way it is, dean, and I don't want to hear anything to the contrary." A large reason Dean Weeks had resigned was his running battle with Wright.

While serving first as assistant and then as associate dean, I had worked very closely with Dean Weeks. I had known firsthand of difficulties between President Wright and Dean Weeks.

Wright's decision turned out well. Corley did well, the school prospered and all of us were pleased.

From the president's decision to name a rookie professor dean of an established and well-known law school and from the ensuing results, I pass this observation to all teachers: Be good to your students, one of them may some day unexpectedly become your boss!

A LAW SCHOOL FIRST

A visiting female Stanford University law professor spent a few hours with us at Cumberland. She noted portraits on the walls of our moot courtroom. "All of them are elderly white males," she said, and that led her to ask about our attitude toward women. Whereupon I told her about Audrey Gaston.

In the middle 1960s, on the occasion I have in mind, the dean had received an application for admission from Mrs. Gaston, whom he identified as a black person. He asked me (I was assistant dean), "What do you think?"

Mrs. Gaston's application showed she was a college graduate and I replied, "Accept her." (A college degree was not at that time an ABA requirement for law school admission.) Dean responded, "I will have to run it by President (Leslie) Wright." Arthur took the application to the president, who told him the matter must be presented to the Board of Trustees. Dean Weeks and President Wright attended the board meeting and the board voted, with one dissent, to accept the application.

Mrs. Gaston attended Cumberland, was graduated and passed the Alabama Bar exam on her first effort. Mrs. Audrey Gaston thus became the first black person admitted to a law school in Alabama, the first to be graduated in the state and, on becoming a member of the Alabama Bar Association, the first black member who had been graduated from a law school in Alabama.

All this occurred without any court action and was made possible by virtue of the actions of an elderly white male, Dean Arthur Weeks, whose portrait hangs on a wall in the Cumberland School of Law. I give Arthur this strong credit: He could have tossed the application in the wastebasket and likely ended the matter.

I was informed in the 1970s that Mrs. Gaston had become the first black female attorney hired in the Southeast as an assistant U.S. Attorney—employed in Birmingham by a white Republican U.S. Attorney, Wayman Sherrer, a Nixon appointee.

While thinking about this historic event another "first" came to mind, albeit only an amusing incident. Mrs. Mabel Fitch was one of four or five female law students enrolled in Cumberland Law School in the mid-1960s. She was not right out of college, but was a good, mature student and personable. We all liked her.

I recall that she was a widow, perhaps 45 or 50 years old.

At the start of her second year she was dissatisfied with the scheduling of the required Equity course, so she went to see Dean Arthur Weeks.

"Dean," she said, "Equity is scheduled at 9 a.m. on Monday, Wednesday, and Friday. For years I have visited my beautician at 9 a.m. on Friday, so I have a problem with attending Equity at an early hour.

Dean Weeks responded, "Mrs. Fitch, what hour do you conclude at the beauty parlor?"

"About eleven."

"I'll see what can be done."

That semester Equity was offered at 9 a.m. on Monday and Wednesday and at noon on Friday. Beauty must be served. I know about this firsthand—I taught the Equity course.

The widow, Mrs. Fitch, a loyal alumna, married the widower, Ingram Beasley, a circuit judge, who was one of Cumberland's adjunct professors.

KEEP TALKING AND SMILE IF POSSIBLE

Dr. Leslie Wright was president of Samford University for a quarter century plus a year, 1957 to 1983. They were years of growth under excellent leadership.

I liked Dr. Wright, although at times he was exasperating. I know that for a long time he felt the same way towards me. One of the gripes I had was his propensity to respond occasionally to an issue without having adequately studied it, as well as periodically being dictatorial. I will explain, but first this: For years, I believed the president envisioned me, Cumberland Law School professor and associate dean, as Dean Arthur Weeks' alter ego. Wright, I'm convinced, believed that whatever Weeks wanted for the law school I strongly supported. He was correct in that belief. That I was loyal to Weeks did not, however, make me disloyal to the president.

The law school's accreditation by the American Bar Association and its membership in the Association of American Law Schools were vitally important, and the dean wanted to keep Cumberland in good standing with both the ABA and the AALS. Further, Weeks sought always to build the law school's reputation in the national community as well as in the local one.

President Wright did not seem to regard the school's reputation as all that important, especially on the national level, and he gave us the impression that he did not understand the importance of the law school's meeting more than the ABA minimum standards of accreditation. He knew we had to remain accredited to stay viable as a law school, but he wanted to cut corners to economize, which put the school in a position of just getting by.

This approach was puzzling because Wright was president when Cumberland was purchased by Howard College and brought from Lebanon, Tennessee, to the Homewood campus in 1961.

Too, there was a time when the president apparently wanted Cumberland to maintain a small enrollment. Once when I was in his office in the late sixties or early seventies, when Cumberland's enrollment was between 200 and 300 and growing, I suggested that Samford should consider a substantial addition to the law building and increasing the enrollment to six or seven hundred.

The president responded promptly, and it seemed to me, without forethought and almost defiantly, "There will never be an addition to the law school." I interpreted that to mean, "Don't bring this up again."

A few years later, by 1974, law school enrollment had reached 600 and our space soon was doubled. We moved into the expansion in 1976, occupying both the former and new building. Since 1974, enrollment has never been below 500 (as I write) and has been as high as 700.

I do not profess to know why President Wright had a change of mind concerning an addition to the law building that was first occupied in January 1964. But two thoughts come to mind: the burgeoning law school enrollment was certainly appealing to him, because tuition dollars rolled in; and, Dean Donald Corley wanted a larger law building and was successfully persuasive.

In addition to the substantial physical plant expansion in 1976, under the leadership of President Wright and Dean Corley, the Beeson Library was built and dedicated in 1998, an $8.6 million addition to the law building. The latter occurred under a different law dean and Dr. Wright's successor, President Thomas Corts.

Professor Donaldson- March 1971

Thinking back now about the law school's early years and President Wright's strong assertiveness, I wonder perhaps if he occasionally questioned my allegiance to him. I was aware that I was considered by my students to be a "tough" and demanding professor. President Wright's two sons, top-quality students whom I liked, were in law school in the late 1960s; perhaps the president viewed my "toughness" with them as a way of getting back at him. Not so, in any way. That would have been totally out of character for me. I would have been pleased had all my students been the quality of the Wright brothers.

With the passing years President Wright mellowed as I clearly revealed my desire to be cooperative, and we developed a very cordial relationship.

Despite our earlier mutual exasperation and some puzzling decisions by the two of us, I see the significance of two persons, on different employment levels, determined to keep communication lines open, making possible a rewarding reconciliation.

Because the law school didn't always get what its leadership wanted, on occasion some of us took issue with the administration. Yet I now look upon Dr. Wright's long reign as revealing him as the man for the times. As president of Howard College, a small Baptist institution, he intended to convert it to a strong Baptist-affiliated university. He succeeded.

Moral: Keep talking. Smile if possible.

PROFESSOR, DON'T KEEP ME FROM COFFEE

During the last week of the semester Cumberland Law School students rate their professors in nine areas. They are encouraged to write anonymous comments on the rating sheets.

The law school dean makes the ratings and comments available to his faculty after the students have received their grades for the semester.

In the past I was rated by the 69 students in my Civil Procedure course. Several of their remarks caught my attention, especially as not one of those student comments had ever appeared on previous ratings.

One student wrote, "The professor won't take no mess off nobody." I'm not sure of the message that was supposed to convey, but it was reliable; there's never been a question as to who's in charge in my classroom.

I basically use the Socratic Method to teach: ask many questions, praise students who make excellent responses, and occasionally praise merely adequate responses. I prod and probe and at times make it plain that a particular response is deficient, that the student could and should do better. A few times during a semester I will say to a student who is unprepared, "Sit down," indicating my displeasure with an unsatisfactory dialogue.

I encourage students to speak whatever is on their minds, to think aloud so that periodically we have lively discussions. Makes me wonder if a non-lawyer stranger to law school teaching were to eavesdrop, he might observe, "If there's a professor in there, he's sure putting up with a mess."

Another student wrote "A professor should not express in class his views opposing abortion." Correct, that is, if the view expressed is unrelated to the course material. I stick close to the subject matter, but I have no qualms stating my opposition to abortion on demand when the subject of abortion is an issue in an assigned case. Such was the circumstance that prompted the student's comment.

Another student penned this: "Professor had no business telling us during a class period that he believes in the Lord Jesus Christ as his Savior." The student was correct — on that occasion I had clearly violated my personal and professional policy to stay on the day's subject matter. I'm not sure what prompted the statement, though something did. If my confession of faith had not simply come out of the blue, and had instead fit snugly in a class discussion, I would not have considered the comment inappropriate. I like to work whatever I deem applicable into discussion of cases.

For example, we have studied an important civil procedure opinion written by former New York Federal Judge Harold Medina. I mentioned that Medina was a federal district court judge when I was an FBI agent in Manhattan in the late 1940s. He later served many years on the court of appeals, lived to 101, even wrote opinions while in his 90s. I take the opportunity, following my reference to the judge's longevity, to point out that Medina worked out regularly, keeping himself physically fit, which helped him handle hard-nosed New York trial lawyers, some of whom in trial were rude, obnoxious and outright stinkers.

Then I remind my class that spiritual exercise is also important for an attorney (and judge) and I refer to my own faith.

The one topic I never discuss in class is politics. I leave my political views for another forum. Unfortunately some law professors in other schools don't practice that.

Perhaps a separate paper should be written on another student's comment: "I hate the course, I hate the professor." I wonder if the student disliked the professor so much that it rubbed off on his efforts in the course. Perhaps the student disliked law school, or protested a father who insisted he attend law school. Or perhaps the comment resulted from the student's exasperating oral performance in class, followed by my tart "sit down."

One student in the Civil Procedure course wrote, "Professor should spend more time discussing theory, not so much time with civil procedure rules." In the same course, on the same day, in another student's evaluation, were these words, "Professor should put more time on the rules, not as much on theory." My interpretation of the foregoing was that perhaps I had theory and the rules pretty much in balance, that is, if the two students' comments represented a class consensus.

These words appeared on a rating sheet: "This professor stands out." He certainly didn't mean, "Stands out" physically; I'm 5'8", weigh 145 pounds and wear a size 39 suit coat.

Ego impels me to include this comment: "Best professor I ever had in my whole career." Now that's standing out! I hope the student thought that after getting his or her semester grade.

A comment I best remember, perhaps because it's the most practical: "The professor frequently talks four or five minutes after the bell rings. With only a 10-minute break between classes, I don't have time for my coffee." I instituted a new policy that gives students their full 10 minutes. Well, usually.

CHEST CLEARANCE

In the early years of my Cumberland Law School professorship I taught Contracts. The six-hour course was offered for freshmen, three hours in the fall and three in spring. Some students considered it tough. I concede few A's were earned each semester.

One of my students who had made an A in the fall in Contracts I made an F in Contracts II in the spring. The following academic year the student repeated Contracts II and passed. Upon graduation he began practicing law in Birmingham and in the ensuing 30 years has done remarkably well.

Several years after his graduation we met at a state bar reception. Bill plainly was a bit inebriated. He dropped an arm over my shoulder and slurred, "Professor, I been meaning to speak to you. Professor, out there at the law school..." he hesitated as if measuring his words, then resumed… "Professor, at Cumberland, you sonofabitch."

"Bill, I'm glad you got that off your chest."

"Me too," he said, dropping his arm and staring at the floor. Then, forcing a grin, he wobbled away.

Not long ago I testified for him in one of his class action lawsuits.

He was recently listed in The Best Lawyers in America.

AN OFFER TO BECOME LAW DEAN ELSEWHERE

When Howard College President Harwell Davis (Major Davis) told me just before my graduation in 1947 that he hoped to see me "come back here some day and teach," he wasn't referring to a law school. Howard did not acquire a law school until 1961.

That year ex-president Davis, Howard College President Leslie Wright and Birmingham attorney Arthur Weeks, a former law school dean, led in bringing the Cumberland School of Law from its original home in Lebanon, Tennessee, to Howard College in Birmingham. Howard would become Samford University in 1965.

I joined the Cumberland law faculty in the summer of 1962 and taught there for 43 years, retiring at the end of the spring term 2005. From 1981 until 1992 I was on leave of absence, serving as U.S. Attorney for the Northern District of Alabama. Even during the leave I regularly taught a law course each Thursday evening.

While at Cumberland I had opportunities to teach elsewhere. On one occasion in 1975 I considered a deanship at Mississippi College.

At that time Mississippi College in Clinton, Mississippi, had decided to acquire and operate the Jackson School of Law, a privately owned law school in Jackson, Mississippi, not accredited by the American Bar Association. Of course the school's president planned to take the steps necessary to obtain full accreditation.

Mississippi College President Lewis Nobles invited me to meet with him and discuss my possibly becoming dean. Patti and I drove from our home in Helena, and one Saturday morning Dr. Nobles and I talked in his campus office from 8 a.m. until noon with neither rising from his chair.

In our conversation he asked what salary I would expect. I replied $30,000. He flinched, saying that as president he was paid $22,500. But he added, "Perhaps I can get a Jackson law firm to put you on the payroll for an additional $7,500. His implication was clear: It would be inappropriate for the Mississippi College law dean to be paid more than the college president. When he referred to a law firm paying a portion of the dean's salary, I saw a red flag.

After Dr. Nobles and I parted company, Patti and I visited our friends Reuben and Eunice Green in Jackson, and then we returned to Helena.

I heard nothing from Nobles for three to four weeks until a call came from the vice-president of Mississippi College offering me the law school deanship. I told him I would call back. Patti and I talked again, although we had earlier decided we were not interested in moving. While Nobles and I had talked, Patti had driven around Clinton and decided, "This place doesn't look any better than Helena." (She was benevolent; to us it didn't look as good.)

A few days after I declined the offer, Major Davis and I sat beside each other in the moot court room of Cumberland during a law program. When it concluded, Major Davis surprised me with a comment I truly appreciated: "I'm glad you did not accept that offer from Mississippi College and will remain here."

I never knew that he had any knowledge of the offer. Many things go on without our knowledge.

Harwell Davis had been widely known as "Major" Davis since World War I. After retiring as president of Howard College, he had pushed to have the name changed to Samford University in honor of his friend Frank Samford, a benefactor of the college.

One day in the early years of Cumberland Law School's move to the Howard campus, the Major and I sat in the jury box in a crowded moot court room attending another of the law school's many programs. Law School Dean Weeks introduced a new assistant professor. Major whispered, "What is his (the new assistant's) salary?" I was assistant dean, hence aware of it, and I told him.

He repeated the amount and added, "That's $2,500 more than I was paid when I became president of Howard College" (in 1939).

ONE PROFESSOR'S VIEW OF FEMALE LAWYERS

Let me confess right up front that for years I've been delighted to see female lawyers enter the legal profession. No doubt one reason is because my oldest daughter, Sharon Donaldson Stuart is one of them — a trial lawyer.

But my delight began early in my teaching career. Several female law students in the 1960s set the tone.

The first four were Mrs. Elizabeth Eshelman, Mrs. Betty Love, Mrs. Carolyn Nelson and Mrs. Joanne Furner.

As related in an earlier chapter, in the spring of 1966 Mrs. Audrey Gaston sought admission to Cumberland. She was accepted, enrolled and did well academically. Our first black student, she not only integrated the Cumberland School of Law, her admission meant that Samford University was integrated.

In 1967 a recent graduate of Judson College arrived on our campus, interested in entering the Cumberland School of Law.

Upon completing her undergraduate studies she desired to attend the Tulane Law School but had been rebuffed by its dean. Mrs. Judith Crittenden, currently a prominent Birmingham attorney and recent president of the Cumberland Law School's National Alumni Association, related to me that in 1967 her interview with the Tulane law school dean resulted in these statements:

DEAN: If we accept you here, you will take a seat from a male applicant and thus prevent that man from attending Tulane.

DEAN: You are a woman, so you probably will marry and not graduate.

DEAN: If you were to graduate, you would not be able to practice law because you won't be hired.

When Mrs. Crittenden interviewed with Dean Weeks at Cumberland, she found he held clearly contrary views about female law students from those held by the Tulane dean. He welcomed her.

The Cumberland dean's desire to accept Mrs. Crittenden also was approved by precedent set long before by the old "gray beards" of Cumberland when the school was still in Lebanon, Tennessee. Cumberland had graduated several women as early as 1906.[1] Twenty-six years later one of my nieces, Dorothy Donaldson, was graduated there after making all A's.

Harvard Law School graduated its first female law students in 1953[2].

Fair-minded and far-sighted leadership has for generations been a hallmark of the Cumberland School of Law.

---

[1] David J. Langum and Howard P. Walthall, From Maverick to Mainstream: Cumberland School of Law, University of Georgia Press, 1997, pg. 90

[2] The National Law Journal, November 23, 1998, pg. B4.

Notwithstanding a law school's policy on admission of women, for many years there was a paucity of them. For that matter there were few women in any law school in the United States until the 1970s. In that decade female law school enrollment mushroomed over the nation.

Today in several law schools 50 percent of the students are women. Enrollment figures (as of this writing) show that almost half of the more than 125,000 students in the American Bar Association approved law schools in the country are women — that's more than 55,000.

And they will keep coming. Without female students most of the 190-plus ABA approved law schools would suffer drastic and immediate downsizing, or admission standards would be lowered. Furthermore, many women are the leading scholars in their classes. That has been a fact for more than 25 years.

I recall that in the late 1970s when Cumberland had only 20 percent female enrollment, a woman was the top academic graduate three out of four years.

The last two times I taught Civil Procedure (1997-98, 2001-02) two women in each class made the highest grades. The same thing occurred frequently in my other courses.

A male law student is reported to have said, referring to a female colleague's high grades, "This is not just embarrassing, it's humiliating."

Within the first quarter of this new century, female lawyers will head up large law firms, handle the toughest courtroom cases, unravel the thorniest legal problems, serve in large numbers as judges, law deans, professors and officeholders. Women will be leading lecturers on legal topics and will be lauded and applauded for their legal skills.

I expect all of those things to occur with civility and a high level of integrity.

ALMOST DEAN?

An unexpected and strange turn of events may have deprived me of a law school deanship at Samford University. Here's how it happened.

In 1970 Bob Dawson, in his senior year, was president of the Cumberland Law School Student Bar Association. He had been in two of my classes and we had become friends.

Congressman Jack Edwards of Mobile called me one day in 1970 and asked if there was a Cumberland student whom I would personally vouch for to be his legislative assistant. The First District congressman noted that he had never employed a legislative assistant, but he wanted to give it a go. Without hesitation I recommended Robert K. Dawson of Scottsboro, Alabama.

Edwards accepted Dawson and the two hit it off so well that near the end of Dawson's employment term, Edwards asked me, "Can you send me another Bob Dawson?"

Bob remained in Washington, rose in favor and ultimately in 1989 became Assistant Secretary of Army for Civil Works under President George Bush. For years he has been eminently successful in the private sector.

Now back to Dawson's senior year at Cumberland. On a Saturday in April 1970, as president of SBA, Bob spoke briefly at the annual Law Day luncheon. He had prepared well, too well for Samford President Leslie Wright.

Bob had taken offense to what he perceived to be a slighting of the law school SBA by Dr. Wright.

I don't recall the precise words of Dawson's complaint, although the substance was that he had made several requests of the Samford administration and had been ignored — given the silent treatment.

To my great surprise the 25-year-old law student—in the presence of an audience of 300, including President and Mrs. Wright, trustee and Federal Judge Hobart Grooms and other dignitaries — said in his soft manner, "I will take this opportunity to thank Dean Donaldson (I was associate dean) for being available during this busy year and giving me valuable advice."

Bob proceeded, in dramatic language, to criticize President Wright. His words were neither vulgar nor profane, but they were forceful.

I cannot quote Bob's descriptive terminology; that is not necessary for a listener then or a reader now to presume that the associate dean, namely me, had counseled Bob.

In retrospect, I believe that Dr. Wright deemed I had made two mistakes. The first was my failure to dash to the podium and defend the president. I could have explained, factually, that during the school year, while Bob and I had talked on many subjects, not once had we discussed his planned comments at the Law Day appearance. I never moved; never said a word. Secondly, when Bob concluded his remarks, I applauded in full view of President and Mrs. Wright.

Dr. Wright was furious; Mrs. Wright's facial expressions showed she was really upset. No surprise.

Monday morning, Law Dean Arthur A. Weeks and I got a call to be in the president's office in an hour. We were there promptly at 9 a.m. Immediately the president told us we were responsible for what he described as Bob Dawson's "egregious conduct."

No explaining on our part was acceptable. He made clear that I should have read the student's prepared remarks or at least should have discussed with him the substance of what he would say. In addition, the president said perhaps I could have suggested he be positive about Samford because important guests would be there.

Dean Weeks and I practiced a bit of mollification, keeping calm, speaking softly, nodding when appropriate, but assuaged not his ruffled feathers.

A couple of years later Dean Weeks resigned. Immediately after Weeks' resignation, President Wright called a meeting of the law faculty and announced the appointment of Don Corley, a second-year member of the faculty, as law dean.

Some faculty members expressed the view that Wright had passed over several of them because he wanted a toady as dean, and who better than a person beginning his second year of teaching? Several of the law faculty were well qualified to be dean. As senior member of the faculty and associate dean, I thought I was the most logical choice. It was not to be.

A quick learner, Don matured rapidly and handled the position with skill and full faculty cooperation until his untimely death in 1984.

Well before Dean Corley's passing, I had become U.S. Attorney for the Northern District of Alabama. Upon my appointment in early 1981, Dr. Wright had forgiven my "transgression;" he disclosed that forgiveness as shown on the facing page:

𝕾𝖆𝖒𝖋𝖔𝖗𝖉 𝖀𝖓𝖎𝖛𝖊𝖗𝖘𝖎𝖙𝖞

𝕭𝖎𝖗𝖒𝖎𝖓𝖌𝖍𝖆𝖒, 𝕬𝖑𝖆𝖇𝖆𝖒𝖆 35209

OFFICE OF THE PRESIDENT

July 7, 1981

Judge Frank Donaldson
107 Lucerne Boulevard
Birmingham, Alabama 35209

Dear Frank:

Upon the recommendation of Dean Corley and Vice President Wheeler, I am happy to grant you a leave of absence from your teaching position in the Cumberland School of Law during the time of your service as U. S. Attorney for the Northern District of Alabama.

All of us are delighted that you received this appointment and we wish for you all possible happiness and success.

With warmest personal regards and all good wishes to you and Pattie, in which Mrs. Wright joins me, I am

Sincerely your friend,

Leslie S. Wright
President

LSW:gck

cc: Dr. R. E. Wheeler
    Dr. Donald E. Corley

𝕿𝖍𝖊 𝕬𝖑𝖆𝖇𝖆𝖒𝖆 𝕭𝖆𝖕𝖙𝖎𝖘𝖙 𝖀𝖓𝖎𝖛𝖊𝖗𝖘𝖎𝖙𝖞

That leave was for 11 years. It is unlikely any university will allow a professor to be away more than a decade and return without a break in service.

Although I had missed out on becoming dean in 1972, 20 years later, by virtue of Wright's letter granting the extended leave, I took advantage of the opportunity and returned to the law school. Soon I was named professor emeritus and taught as such until retirement in May 2005.

Without Wright's letter my return to teaching at Cumberland and becoming professor emeritus would have never happened; the 11-year absence would have been a barrier.

I hasten to add that Bob Dawson and I remain friends; I hope the time will come when he will be a member of the president's cabinet, the U.S. President, that is.

THE PROF'S SPY

Some 40 years ago law professor Charles Kelso at Indiana University, and a representative of the Association of American Law Schools (AALS) visited my Contracts class at Cumberland. I use the word "visited" loosely as Kelso never entered the room. During the session of which I write, he sat in a chair in the hallway near the back door of the classroom. Since the room's door was open he could hear what was said by my students and me. I did not know he was there; didn't know he was on campus nor planning a visit.

After class he spoke with me briefly, was praiseworthy in his remarks and advised he was doing a survey "judging" law professors' performances ("judging" my term). Kelso said he had visited dozens of classrooms — that my class performance was in the top 10, perhaps the best class session he had attended.

Kelso explained he expected to show a movie of outstanding American law teachers at a forthcoming AALS annual conference. He asked me to film one of my classes and send the film to him to analyze.

Several weeks went by and I did nothing about his request. He called. I explained that (as he knew) I used the Socratic Method of teaching, not strictly lecture, and it was impractical for me to film the class session with the equipment I had. Whereupon he suggested the class discussion be filmed anyway it could be done, and please mail him the tape.

I did so, but microphones for recording purposes were not placed in several spots throughout the room for the students to use. On the day selected I invited one of my students to come to the front of the room. He and I discussed one case for the full class period. The whole session was a dud. I didn't do well, the class was indifferent, feeling left out, there were few questions, fewer comments, no enthusiasm, poor filming. It dawned on me afterwards I used the wrong case for the occasion. What a flop. Then I topped it all off by mailing Kelso the film. Result? Kelso called. He didn't say he recognized a lemon when he saw one; he did not need to, but rather expressed his view that the class was dull, and appeared contrived. End of best American law teacher. Which leads me to digress: In my 43 years of law professoring I never once went to class unprepared. Not that I was motivated to show off in front of students, but I had a keen desire to teach, to teach well, and to always be a hop, skip and jump ahead of the brightest and most studious of those students sitting before me. My view has always been that preparedness is intimately associated with professionalism.

But, I believe that once I blew an oral argument before an appellate court and once during a lecture I really missed the boat before a group of lawyers. The oral argument was done when I was in private practice and simply squeezed too thin. Preparation, preparation, preparation. It's number one and number one was lacking. A solo practitioner, I had too many irons in the fire. That was my excuse then, which is no excuse. Sorry.

There was also the embarrassment at the lecture. I bombed and knew it. Self-consciousness also occurred when I noticed a guest in the room, the most knowledgeable expert on my topic in the United States. We were in Montgomery in February 1973 at the mid-winter meeting of the Alabama State Bar. I had prepared my remarks but had gotten in over my head. I'm reasonably certain many Alabama lawyers present did not detect my weakness, but our out-of-state guest, the national expert on the subject, no doubt thought, "What is going on here?" I felt later I had not misled anyone, but was certain I had not been helpful.

I didn't drown, but swallowed a lot of water. From that experience I learned to swim. A year later I addressed an audience of about 300 Alabama lawyers on the same general topic, spoke for 90 minutes, and felt comfortable with my remarks. When the session ended, a highly respected state circuit court judge spoke kindly to me, "That was the best legal presentation I've ever heard." Can't top that. I wish that I could have redeemed myself with Professor Charles Alan Wright, who only a few months before sat through my embarrassment at the bar meeting.

Back to Professor Kelso and the Best Law Teachers in America.

The Contracts class I conducted that Kelso liked was not one I considered the best. In one class (during the same academic year Kelso visited) my Contracts students and I discussed two cases with very similar facts with opposite results. The cases involved two different state appellate court opinions, one court writing a decision favoring the winning plaintiff, the other court laying down the law on behalf of the prevailing defendant. The circumstances of the parties in each instance were substantially identical.

My students were unusually well prepared. The dialogue was as good as it gets.

One other brief aside: A short time ago my students and I had the most spirited class discussion ever in my career. There were 20 upper class students, 18 of whom were seniors. The students were excited, voices were raised, at times before one student concluded her remarks another one began talking. They chose sides, unplanned, with no nudging from me. Near the end of the 75-minute class period I held up both arms, palms facing the students, speaking with a reasonably elevated voice, called out, "Hey, hey," and with a big grin, "this class is out of control."

I later thought that if Kelso were sitting outside the room he would surely want it to be filmed. However, a stranger, especially to law teaching, overhearing the students, would have wondered if a professor was present, and very likely believed, "that class is out of control."

I loved it — but ought never have turned raised palms to the students. Contra. My arms should have been outstretched with both thumbs up! And I should have thanked them for their robust discussion, all of it on point.

Again, return to Kelso: At the annual AALS conference he showed two films, one I don't recall, other than it dealt with a subject I didn't teach. In the second film a female Contracts professor and her students were shown in a good, lively discussion of the two cases I referred to above that I deem to have been my favorite class session. Sure, I should have filmed it. Kelso would have liked it had the photography been done expertly. More importantly, I would like to have preserved it.

SHERMAN OAK, ONCE REMOVED

As part of Samford University homecoming of 1999, a group of us planted an oak sapling on campus at Talbird Circle. We planted an offspring of Sherman Oak, a longtime resident of the Howard College campus in East Lake. About 2003 it was transplanted in front of Samford Hall just below what is now the president's office.

Howard had moved from East Lake to Homewood in 1957 and eight years later was renamed Samford University. Sherman Oak remained behind because transplanting a 75-year-old tree was not practical.

In the 1990s lightening hit Sherman Oak and ruined it, but not before it had poured forth sufficient acorns to produce a bunch of saplings, one of which was brought to Talbird Circle on October 30, 1999.

Most Howard alumni have fond memories of Sherman Oak, which by the way was a southern red oak. For years, word is that on many occasions marriage proposals, even sweet nothings, were whispered beneath its rich green leaves.

A concrete bench was firmly fixed beneath Sherman Oak and I recall sitting there one evening beside a Howard coed discussing something lofty, probably demilitarization. Well, why not? WWII had recently ended.

Tall tales abound about goings-on 'neath the famous oak. One such tale is that a student was seen sitting under Sherman with a textbook, but that has never been confirmed.

At our homecoming on that clear, pleasant October morning, my wife Patti and I were among several Samford graduates who spaded dirt around the roots of Sherman Junior. In other words, several of us planted the sapling.

After the ceremony I mentioned to Patti that I hoped the ancient chef's quip, "Too many cooks spoil the broth" wouldn't apply. As in "Too many planters killed the little tree." That didn't happen; the tree flourished. But, alas, it was transplanted after a few years and is now located at the northeast front of Samford Hall.

The oak continues to thrive and is more than 20 feet tall.

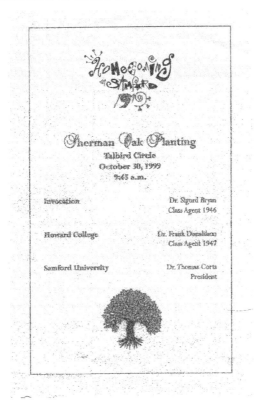

GRITS IN ABUNDANCE

For many years law professors in schools that are members of the Association of American Law Schools have met annually. Those of us who teach in law schools in the southeastern U.S. have a special breakfast get-together.

It is our practice to communicate to the chef that we want grits served with our ham and eggs. On one such occasion we met in Washington, D.C.

At breakfast our gathering of 40 or 50 people, as requested, was served grits. About halfway through the meal a waiter came in with a large bowl of grits and a ladle. He moved table to table serving the grits and urged us all to have a second helping.

When he came to our table and made his second helping suggestion, one of our group responded, "You have a lot of grits, do you?"

The waiter stopped dead in place. "Have we! You won't believe what happened."

And, of course, he told us. That morning the cook had gotten our message to cook grits; trouble was the man had never cooked grits. He asked for help and one of his co-workers found a maid from the Deep South who knew how to cook them. "But," said the waiter, "she didn't tell the cook the grits would swell."

We anticipated his punch line: "Man, we got enough grits in that kitchen to feed the city of Washington!"

Assistant Dean Frank W. Donaldson,
LL.B., 1954, University of Alabama

SOMEBODY SAY POLITICS?

They didn't say it is a bumpy road full of potholes.

THE REPUBLICAN CANDIDATE

President Reagan, once questioned about having changed his political party affiliation, responded that he didn't leave the Democratic Party, that the Democratic Party left him.

I cannot say that I was ever a democrat, although for most of the first two-thirds of the 20th Century Alabama was a one-party state, and that one party was not Republican. To vote in either statewide or local contests and have that vote count meant voting for a democrat candidate.

Until 1964 Republicans fielded few candidates and none won statewide or congressional races. Then Republican presidential candidate Barry Goldwater broke the democrat monopoly in Alabama, and Alabamians won several state and federal offices.

I had been waiting 20 years for the breakthrough. My first vote in any election, in 1944, was for Republican presidential candidate Thomas E. Dewey, who opposed Franklin D. Roosevelt's attempt for a fourth straight term. I was in service in 1944 and voted an absentee ballot. As we all know, FDR won.

I had not been fond of FDR, having looked with disfavor as he attempted to pack the Supreme Court, and at his administration's heavy-handed action during the Depression in killing off hogs (to raise prices for growers) while millions of Americans went hungry. I also wondered how President Roosevelt and his military advisors could not have been aware of impending tragedy at Pearl Harbor.

The year 1964 stirred my own political interest. I thought seriously of trying for an elective office in 1966 as a Republican, then decided to hold off for a couple more years until the next presidential election.

In 1968 Alabama's Fifth Congressional District included all of Shelby County, where I lived, as well as nine other counties, mostly Black Belt, and a portion of west Jefferson County.

Early that year I pondered a race as a Republican for the U.S. House of Representatives. I knew that without a political fluke, I would not win. I expressed that view to my wife and privately to a couple of close friends. However, I thought such a race would be an interesting and worthwhile experience.

More importantly, I believed that republicans should not be reluctant to run for office no matter the odds, candidates would help build the party. I earnestly believed that the Republican Party's day would come in Alabama.

When my Cumberland Law School boss, Dean Arthur Weeks, swung a sabbatical for me, I qualified as a Republican Party congressional candidate in the Fifth District. So did five others.

Sure enough, I was soundly defeated, coming in third. Walter Flowers, a democrat from Tuscaloosa, won handily. William McKinley Branch of Eutaw was second and thereby made history: A black man in an Alabama race for Congress came in ahead of four white men. I had become the first white major party office-seeker in the 20th Century to finish behind a black candidate in Alabama. Branch went on to become probate judge in Greene County. I went back to teaching at Cumberland Law School.

Unusually tough political misfortune had dogged me in the campaign. Please don't misunderstand; even if I had had unimaginably good fortune, I still would have taken a shellacking.

Among the reasons: raising money to finance a campaign in 11 counties with approximately 500,000 residents was as tough as getting blood from the proverbial turnip. So there was precious little money for advertisements.

The National Republican Party had promised me $10,000 if I would qualify and run. I never saw a penny of it—an outright broken promise. On my own I never raised $10,000.

I even returned a corporate check that I deemed inappropriate to use. I asked my friend and loyal campaign helper

John Wideman to take the check, as large as any I had received, back to the company president. I said, "John, please say thanks for me and explain that a corporate campaign check is illegal."

He did so. On returning, John displayed the company president's personal check for the same amount as the one returned. He said the president told him, "I always write corporate checks to candidates. Never before has one been returned."

On a trip to Washington I invited presidential candidate Richard Nixon to come to Alabama and make at least one speech for me. He declined, no doubt writing off Alabama because of the "Wallace for President" hysteria. Stupid as the idea was, Alabama voter interest focused on George's third-party race. The Wallace campaign in Alabama was unbelievably strong, sucking up dollars like a whirlwind sucks up straw.

That year the Wallace fantasy ran deep into the boondocks. At a Centreville Fair an elderly woman, upon learning who I was, held a "Wallace for President" brochure in my face, put a finger on George's nose and asked me, "Are you fer him?" She wasted her vote on George as others wasted their votes on me.

Further campaign misfortune occurred in a surprising and irksome way. Media sometimes are criticized for slanting the news or reporting inaccurately, but not for giving the silent treatment to a major-party candidate in a congressional campaign. That happened to me.

In the counties comprising the mostly Black Belt area of the district were several weekly newspapers with countywide circulation. Two of those papers never mentioned my name. I sent them news releases, but not one word of those releases was printed in those two county papers. The other papers seldom mentioned my candidacy and didn't bother to report on the one campaign speech I made in their area.

A candidate can't expect to do well at the polls when ignored by the local press.

Arizona Congressman Morris Udall, in his book, <u>Too Funny to be President</u>, recalled that once during a campaign he poked his head in a barbershop and announced that he was running for president. The barber replied, "Yeah, I know. We were laughing about it just this morning."

I wish I could have gotten that much response in West Alabama, for there my candidacy really didn't seem to exist.

One October morning in Fairfield I introduced myself to a man on the sidewalk. "Where've you been?" he asked, which I interpreted to mean, "It's October and I've never heard of you." I suppose he had been having lunch regularly with the other five candidates.

California Governor Ronald Reagan cut a TV campaign tape for me, but I was so strapped for money I was able to air it only a few times. (I don't know where the tape is today. It was last shown in Tuscaloosa.)

Mention of Governor Reagan reminds me of his visit to Birmingham during my 1968 campaign. The then-governor had been invited to downtown Boutwell Auditorium to boost the

Republican Party and to help raise funds for those of us seeking elective office. By coming here he also was building his own political base in Alabama as he was doing elsewhere. I recall that nonetheless the party had to foot the $8,000 travel expense for his private aircraft.

Several of us candidates were allotted a few minutes to address the audience at Boutwell. As I stood to speak I was quietly informed that Governor Reagan had just arrived and was waiting behind the curtain to speak. So I cut my remarks short, telling the audience (which was unaware Reagan had arrived) that I was signing off early because "a possible future President of the United States is standing in the wings, ready to come dancing on." He seemed pleased with my remark.

Later that evening Governor Reagan hosted a reception at which guests who had paid $100 could greet him and shake hands. I went to the reception expecting to speak with the governor, only to be told that I could not enter the room where he was because I had not paid the $100. "But I'm a candidate for Congress," I said. The doorkeeper was adamant; "Nobody gets in to see the governor without paying the money."

Whooey! As a candidate, I was one of the reasons Ronald Reagan had come to Alabama. I walked away and went home. Actually I already had a close-up photo made in Washington, D.C., as I shook hands with the California governor, as well as with New York Governor Nelson Rockefeller and former Vice President

Richard Nixon. They had spoken at a gathering of Republican congressional candidates from across the country.

For those photos there was no charge!

Oh yes, my campaign for Congress: Unfortunately it went so badly I didn't even win my home county. Although a couple of Republicans had been elected during Senator Barry Goldwater's sweep of Dixie in 1964, "Republican" was still a dirty word in Shelby County and the rest of the district.

I got so few votes a friend suggested I might consider getting a pistol permit.

At home, wife Patti's joking comment about my campaign summed it up, "Any white man who runs for a seat in the House of Representatives as a Republican in Alabama's Black Belt hasn't got enough sense to be in Congress."

The outcome of the race worked out well for me after all. My wife and boys had made it plain that even if I won, they weren't moving to Washington D.C.

Afterthought: It's gratifying to believe that I had a part, small as it was, in helping build the Republican Party in Alabama. I know that when Granddaddy plowed the back 40, first he had to get the mule out of the barn.

IN THE ARENA

I was elected to political office following my first political campaign—and soundly beaten in my next one. Further possible campaigns didn't entice me to be a candidate.

Actually I won my first two political campaigns, that is, if you count election as president of the Howard College student body in 1946. The only public office success was election as Helena, Alabama, town councilman in 1960. A total of 72 votes were sufficient for victory.

In those days a councilman received no pay, service was strictly pro bono publico. During the four-year term I served, we voted that councilmen taking office after the next election be paid five dollars for each meeting attended. I'm not certain whether being on time for a meeting was required.

The outcome of my 1968 race for Congress was less auspicious than the race for Town Council. I got tromped big time in running as a Republican in Alabama's then Fifth Congressional District, comprised substantially of Black Belt counties.

The congressional race cured me of further efforts to seek elective office, although I have tried to help other Alabamians in different races, such as Jefferson County Commission, Birmingham City Council, Shelby County district attorney, Alabama attorney general, U.S. Senate, Alabama Supreme Court and U.S. House of Representatives.

In the last mentioned race I was campaign manager for Mike King, a young lawyer I had known since his birth. His campaign for the June, 1992 primary coincided nicely with my departure as U.S. attorney in March of that year.

Although Mike grew up in Shelby County (part of Shelby was in his campaign district), he had been away from Alabama several years practicing law in New York City and had returned to Alabama's Sixth Congressional District as a resident several months before the election.

I knew, absent a miracle, he could not win, and that few miracles occur in the political arena.

Nonetheless I accepted Mike's request to be his campaign manager. I had developed pretty fair name identification as U.S. Attorney and we hoped to parlay that into votes. It didn't parlay. Maybe I helped him get a few votes, but he needed a lot more than a few.

Considering how badly he was socked, not even close to a runoff in a race with several candidates, one might argue his candidacy would have been better off if I had had no public part in it. On the other hand, Mike could not have won even had a top-drawer professional managed his campaign.

Too bad. Mike is congressional material and would have competently represented constituents in Alabama's Sixth District.

Mike's campaign and those of his adversaries were low key. How very different from the most hotly contested race in which I had input (though my overall role was brief and meager): the contest for chief justice of the Alabama Supreme Court in 1994. There, the chief justice, Sonny Hornsby, a Democrat, and his

Republican challenger, Perry Hooper, Sr., squared off in a race that unfortunately drew nationwide publicity.

During that campaign I actively worked against a sitting chief justice. The chief was a bright, likeable person and no doubt qualified, but I thought it important a change be made.

Contender Hooper and I had become acquainted in 1968 when he ran for the U.S. Senate and I for the House. No Republican had been elected Alabama Chief Justice in the 20th Century. There were other reasons, not necessary to discuss, that I supported the challenger.

The real rhubarb in the 1994 court race revolved around whether certain absentee ballots should be counted or discarded. Several lawsuits were filed following the general election in November. Hooper prevailed but was not sworn in until several months after the election. Ordinarily the winner goes into office in January following the November balloting.

I hope the problems of the kind we saw in that race never crop up again. I don't think they will. However, on the date I write this, Alabama's absentee ballot laws still need repair. They're too lax and too easily manipulated. Perhaps our single most important election law need is a good system of voter identification. I understand such a bill may soon be in the legislative mill. Getting a really good one passed may not be easy. So far, legislation has been flat out weak.

A POLITICAL MYSTERY

In 1996 I was an Alabama delegate to the National Republican Party Convention pledged to Senator Robert Dole. Although Dole possesses many fine qualities, I might just as well have been pledged to a fence post. But I won't go into that.

Twenty-three delegates were to have been chosen by voters statewide and 21 from our seven congressional districts. I signed on for place five in the statewide contest (at-large), which at the time had a qualified candidate, the chairman of the Alabama Republican Party.

The qualifying fee was $150. That became my total expense for the campaign. I considered running a few newspaper ads, but spending money for advertisements would have required additional paperwork to comply with contest rules, so I opted to do nothing that would cost money. Sometimes when chatting with friends I mentioned my interest in making the trip to the convention in San Diego.

The voting took place in the Republican Party primary in June. The media did not run the results of the delegate contests (or if they ran, I missed them), and I didn't hear anything about the outcome for two or three days until a man in Governor Fob James' office called and said I had come in second to the governor in total votes received by the candidates. I had gotten 70,000 plus, the governor many more.

I had won place five with a big margin over my opponent and had received several thousand more votes than the third highest vote getter. Why? The mystery remains.

If I had been a delegate in 1992, four years earlier, and had won, there would have been no mystery. Widespread name identification, especially in the heavily Republican area of the state, would have explained the vote, for I had been in the news regularly and prominently several months just prior to leaving office as U.S. Attorney in March 1992. The publicity resulted from an investigation of a local politician (another story).

Was it likely the public attention from one of the top Birmingham stories in 1992 would have propelled a Republican candidate into a big victory four years later? No.

Perhaps a few articles I wrote for <u>The Birmingham News</u> (Sunday edition) during those four years had generated voter interest. But not that much.

Perhaps my position on the ballot, five spots from the top, coupled with my name appearing alphabetically ahead of my opponent's name did the trick. But that doesn't necessarily explain the large vote-margin over the place six candidate, the one directly below me on the ballot.

Then there's the possibility that approximately 11 years as U.S. Attorney for the Northern District of Alabama left its mark. During that time a number of high-profile news items were published. And in my last nine years in office I made 375 speeches throughout North Alabama. Perhaps those speeches influenced the ballot count.

Twenty-eight years earlier, in 1968, I had run as a candidate for the U.S. House. Did that help in 1996? No way, except for a handful of votes from friends of that era.

So again the question: Why the big vote?

The mystery remains.

WHY JACKASSES RUN

Shortly after Joe Jasper, my friend and former law school classmate at the University of Alabama, decided to seek a seat in the Alabama House of Representatives, he asked me to make a talk on his behalf. I agreed, did so, and included in my remarks a story usually attributed to Abe Lincoln.

Seems a king of old loved to hunt but invariably got rained on each time he went into the field. Because rain was so persistent on the days he hunted, he became aggravated and sought out prophets, other wise men, soothsayers, and fortune-tellers, anyone who might forecast the weather accurately so that he could hunt without getting wet.

They all failed, so he put out a national notice that he would make the one who could accurately predict the weather ruler over half the realm.

Shortly someone told the king that in the outer reaches of his kingdom lived an old farmer who could call it right. The king sent for the farmer/forecaster, who told the king he could hunt Tuesday and Thursday of the following week and remain dry on those days.

The king hunted those days and stayed dry, so he again called for the farmer. "I promised," the king said, "that the one saving me from the rain would be made ruler over half my kingdom."

The farmer quickly responded, "Sire, it is not I who predicts the weather; it is my donkey."

"So," replied the king, "Whoever, whatever!" Whereupon he made the donkey ruler over half his kingdom.

"Ever since that time, every jackass wants an office."

Joe Jasper failed in his bid for the State House. However, a few years later, the governor named Joe to be a circuit court judge. In that position Judge Jasper served many meritorious years, meaning he stood for re-election several times. But not once, ever again, did he ask me to make another talk for him. Furthermore, I don't recall his ever asking me again to do anything in support of his campaigns. And he was always successful.

I've said many times I'm the world's worst politician. It's a sure bet Joe Jasper agrees.

THE RECRUITER

As a member of the Alabama Republican Party executive committee, I was asked in 1972 to chair the candidate recruitment committee and to make a special effort to line up a candidate or two for an Alabama Supreme Court race. I struck out.

One of the lawyers I urged to run for a place on the court, James Hancock, said he had no interest in such a campaign. His decision was easy for me to understand. After all, the pay was only $22,000 a year, and a justice at that time was expected to live in Montgomery; Hancock lived in Birmingham.

A year later (1973) James Hancock and Foy Guin became federal judges in Birmingham, appointed by Republican President Richard Nixon on the recommendation of John Buchanan, our then Sixth District congressman. (At this writing, both judges still sit on the bench — in senior status.)

Not long after the congressman's judicial recommendations, Buchanan visited the Cumberland Law School as one of our many guest speakers. After his talk to the students and faculty, law Dean Arthur A. Weeks invited Buchanan and me to the dean's office for chitchat, but more than chitchat occurred.

Very outspoken, the dean addressed Buchanan on a subject the dean and I had discussed a short time earlier.

Dean Weeks: "John, don't you think it would be good to put out the word that no lawyer in Alabama can expect to become a federal judge unless that lawyer has campaigned for a state judicial office?"

Buchanan seemed taken aback. He bristled and indicated the dean was attempting to tell him how to do his job. He huffed out of the office.

Arthur said to me, "The congressman seemed to think I had suggested something immoral."

Several years later, in 1980, Congressman Buchanan lost to Albert Lee Smith in the spring Republican primary, Buchanan having lost favor among many of his former supporters, I being one of them.

No congressman fit the Republican mold better than Albert Lee Smith, a truly fine Christian gentleman in every sense of the word. Unfortunately Albert Lee served only one term, losing to a Democrat, who in turn was unseated by a Republican 10 years later.

In early 1981 Congressman Smith and Senator Jeremiah Denton recommended me to President Reagan to be U.S. Attorney for the Northern District of Alabama. I wondered when Reagan made the nomination, if perchance he recalled that 13 years earlier he had cut a TV tape for me in support of my campaign for congress.

UNITES STATES ATTORNEY

The goal of the U.S. Attorney in both civil and criminal cases: "That justice shall be done."

THE SURPRISE

Shortly after former California Governor Ronald Reagan was elected president in November 1980, I got a telephone call from Carl Robinson, M.D./J.D., Bessemer, Alabama, one of my former law students.

"I hope you are interested in becoming U.S. Attorney," Carl said.

"What? It hasn't entered my mind," I replied.

Two or three weeks later Carl called again. "Changed your mind about the U.S. attorney position?"

"No."

"Well," Carl said, "don't dismiss it out of hand. You fit that slot."

Carl pointedly reminded me that the November, 1980 election meant that the White House would change political parties, giving the new president 93 U.S. attorney appointments, including one for the northern district of Alabama.

The chief executive's announcement of his choice of U.S. Attorney for the Northern District of Alabama could be expected a month or two after his swearing in January 20, 1981.

I followed Carl's suggestion and did not dismiss the position "out of hand." I began to think about it and pondered the pros and cons of the job. However, I did nothing else; that is, I made no move toward acquiring the appointment.

My phone rang again. This time the caller was Albert Lee Smith, our local Republican congressman. "Can you meet me for breakfast Saturday morning?"

"Sure," I answered. "Be pleased to do so."

We ate at the Kopper Kettle at Brookwood Mall, had an enjoyable session, and I came away thinking that Congressman Smith well might recommend me for the job to Senator Jeremiah Denton.

That's what happened. Senator Denton sent my name to President Reagan.

Little did I know of events that reportedly were taking place behind the scenes, efforts to try to prevent my nomination. Then at home one evening I got a call from a prominent federal officeholder, advising me that pressure was being put on certain federal officials to stymie my nomination by the president. A particular effort was said to be underway in the Department of Justice in Washington to halt the nomination process for U.S. Attorney in the Northern District of Alabama.

The following event seemed to me to lend plausibility to my informer's report: Early one Saturday morning a man tapped on my office window at the Cumberland Law School. I was trying to work without interruption, but I motioned for the window-tapper to enter the building.

A small black man I figured to be in his late sixties introduced himself. He said he would like for us to chat and we talked for about a half hour.

I don't recall the man's pitch, but I presumed he was a plant, wired and recording every word, so I spoke with measured caution. I neither saw nor heard from him again, nor did any evidence ever surface that he had visited me.

If an effort was being made to stymie my nomination it soon ceased. In February the White House announced that I was the president's choice.

From the time a president is elected until his own appointed U.S. attorney is confirmed usually takes seven to ten months, especially if it's a president's first term. There are hundreds of executive department appointments, each of which requires a full-field FBI background check.

I was sworn in about four months prior to Senate confirmation. This early-entry duty was made possible by the resignation of J.R. Brooks, the competent young official I was replacing, and by a statute that provided for a court-appointed U.S. attorney. The statute has been amended so that today it is the attorney general, not federal judges, who makes an initial interim appointment.

On Friday, May 29, I called Chief Federal Judge Frank McFadden and asked for a court appointment as U.S. attorney. I told him that my duties for the academic year at Cumberland would end on May 31, the day U.S. Attorney Brooks was to resign. The judge had only one question, "Any skeletons in your closet?"

"No, Judge."

I was sworn in on Monday, June 1, 1981.

Immediately upon assuming office I saw and felt uneasiness among several employees. An assistant U.S. attorney had sought the position before I was nominated. As a well-liked intelligent lawyer, he had had the support of many office personnel. Understandably they were disappointed that their colleague had lost out to a law professor known to only a few of the 19 attorneys in the office.

There was a tension I was anxious to dispel, but that dispelling took months. A few resignations and hiring of new personnel sped the healing. So did a fast-growing workload that kept us all busy.

Of course, the passage of time also softened disappointment.

THE UNITED STATES ATTORNEY
CELEBRATING A DAB OF HISTORY

I was sworn in on June 1, 1981 and had the good fortune to serve until March 4, 1992, the second longest tenure as U.S. Attorney in the Northern District of Alabama. One other official served 12 years; I was told he committed suicide in office, so I guess serving about 11 years was sufficient.

It was my good fortune to be in office when the U.S. attorneys celebrated their bicentennial, commemorating the passage of the Judiciary Act Sept. 24, 1789, and 200 years of federal service.

In September 1989, the Executive Office for the United States Attorneys published a slick-cover paperback book for the occasion, Bicentennial Celebration of the United States Attorneys. (I mailed a copy to several local libraries.)

The publication begins with a quotation from Berger v. United States, 295 U.S. 88 (1935), by Justice Sutherland.

"The United States Attorney is the representative not of an ordinary party to a controversy, but of a sovereignty whose obligation to govern impartially is as compelling as its obligation to govern at all; and whose interest, therefore, in a criminal prosecution is not that it shall win a case, but that justice shall be done."

As such, he is in a peculiar and very definite sense the servant of the law, the twofold aim of which is that guilt shall not escape or innocence suffer."

Dick Thornburgh, the 76th U.S. Attorney General, in his letter <u>To the United States Attorneys on Occasion of their 200th Birthday</u>," wrote,

"On September 24, 1789, the Judiciary act was passed establishing the Office of the United States Attorneys — two days later President George Washington commissioned the original thirteen distinguished United States Attorneys. Today, the United States Attorney serves as the chief law enforcement officer in each of the ninety-four districts — for the past two hundred years United States Attorneys have been in the forefront in our nation's history."

Alabama became a state in 1819 and its first U.S. attorney took office a year after, at which time the state comprised one judicial district.

For many years there have been 93 U.S. attorneys serving 94 districts, Alabama having three of the districts with three U.S. attorneys. (The Far Pacific has two districts with one U.S attorney serving both).

The bicentennial book contains highlights from the Office of U.S. Attorneys, including a copy of an October 20, 1882 indictment returned in the Northern District of Alabama against Jesse James and his gang (pages 20-25).

There is also a story about a grateful man who willed his entire estate of $300,000 to Uncle Sam. He died in February 1984. As U.S. attorney, my office did the legal work for the former immigrant's estate. His will expressed his gratitude for life in this great nation. The Birmingham News published the story in early February 1984. The Associated Press picked up the story, which resulted in a friend sending me an AP clipping from The Grand Rapids Press (Michigan) dated February 12, 1984, captioned, "Grateful Alabamian Leaves His All to U.S. Government."

For several generations U.S. Attorneys were on a fee system, resulting in some of them earning huge sums of money, none of it subject to federal income taxation. The Internal Revenue Service had not come into existence. But, long before my service, Congress axed the fee system and devised a fixed pay plan for all U.S. attorneys.

A MIGHT-HAVE BEEN

The following account may appear self-serving. Nonetheless it happened, so I share it.

In 1983 President Ronald Reagan invited the 93 U.S. attorneys to visit the White House. The visit was enjoyable, no question, but I came away a bit frustrated at the time and, in view of what happened, wonder even today about a might-have-been.

The president met with us July 13 in the large second-floor dining room. The huge dining table that many tourists see had been removed, replaced by 93 chairs for the U.S. attorneys, one for Attorney General William French Smith, several others for Department of Justice subordinates, and two for White House staffers.

When we entered the room I told John Bell, U.S. Attorney colleague from Montgomery, that I wanted to sit next to an aisle. I anticipated the president would use that aisle as he made his way to the front of the group; if not then, perhaps as he departed.

John was curious and I explained, "If I get the chance, I would like to express to the president my concern for the safety of our Marines barracked in Beirut, Lebanon." I had studied Middle East history for more than 30 years (on my own), and I told John that it would not surprise me if a "kamikaze" pilot flew his plane, carrying explosives, into the Marine barracks with tragic results. Furthermore, I believed there was no way a few courageous Marines could bring peace to a region that had experienced bloodshed for 3,000-plus years.

President Reagan spoke for about 15 minutes, then after handshakes with some of my colleagues on the front row, he left the room. I had guessed wrong on the aisle he would use, thus I missed any chance of expressing to him my concern about the safety of our military personnel.

A short time later a kamikaze truck loaded with explosives drove into their barracks killing 241 Marines.

Of course, I have no idea how the president might have responded to my concern had I been able to communicate it to him. Nevertheless, I deeply regretted, and do yet, that I missed an opportunity to speak briefly with him.

Years later I learned that Defense Secretary Caspar Weinberger had urged the president not to deploy and house the

Marines in what Weinberger felt was a hazardous area. But other, well-meaning advisers prevailed.

BONDING WITH THE ATTORNEY GENERAL

The 75th Attorney General of the United States had capable people in the Department of Justice so that department business was carried on satisfactorily during his tenure, notwithstanding the media barrage against him the last few months of his term.

Ed Meese did not try to micro-manage. He had great confidence in the abilities of his U.S. attorneys and he let us do our work without looking over our shoulders.

Law officers liked Meese and understandably so. He was as pro-law enforcement as an attorney general could be and was keen on promoting cooperation among federal, state, and local law enforcement personnel.

Like President Ronald Reagan, Attorney General Meese enjoyed humor, especially jokes that would take only a minute or so to tell. As I likewise enjoy verbal fun, I became the unofficial joke-teller at our Attorney General's Advisory Committee meetings. We opened each meeting with my attempt to give everyone a good chuckle.

Occasionally committee members met for dinner. One evening we had an enjoyable meeting just outside Washington, D.C., at the home of Larry McWhorter, at that time Director of the

Executive Office of United States Attorneys. On that occasion Attorney General Meese joined us.

After dinner Meese and five of us sat at a round table in Larry's dining room. For an hour we told jokes. It was a truly delightful evening.

If there is doubt about humor helping us to get to know and like one another, I would like to try dispelling it. One evening ten years after Meese left office, he spoke in Birmingham at The Club. President Reagan was being honored there in absentia.

Shortly after Meese entered the room where several hundred people were gathered, Patti and I went over to greet him. As I neared, he turned, saw me, smiled and exclaimed, "Frank." He put out his hand to greet Patti and me as if he had been looking for us.

ED MEESE AND THE ATTORNEY GENERAL'S ADVISORY COMMITTEE

Not long after being sworn in as a United States Attorney, I asked Bill Tyson, Director of the Executive Office for the U.S. Attorneys, to place me on the attorney general's Advisory Committee.

The 15-member committee still included several appointees of President Carter, so I knew there soon would be a number of openings. Tyson denied my request at that time. However, he did recommend me to the attorney general nearly four years later and I joined the committee in 1985.

The usual term of a committee member was three years, but because of unusual circumstances the slot I filled was for four years. The timing was excellent because I was able to serve on the committee under three attorneys general.

The committee met with the attorney general every two to three months so that I was with William French Smith twice, all meetings for three years with Ed Meese, and two meetings with Dick Thornburgh. (I would like to have had at least one meeting with Attorney General Bill Barr for I hardly knew him.)

As a result of my three years on the committee with Meese we became reasonably well acquainted. I grew to like him and so did my colleagues.

In the summer of 1988 Meese was under investigation by an independent counsel and was being hit hard by the media at every turn. He continued to do his work and appeared upbeat when we were with him, although I have no doubt the constant pounding and hounding took a toll on him. Those days had to be unusually difficult for the attorney general, a top-quality public servant.

So, one morning at the initial assembly of the Advisory Committee we decided that we would show Meese our solid support. He had not seen us for two or three months and I'm sure was not certain of our response to the media blitz against him.

Our meetings were held in a large room next to the attorney general's office. We sat around a long and magnificent table in the center of the room. When Attorney General Ed Meese entered we stood and vigorously applauded.

Meese was delighted. He was not one who customarily showed public emotion, but he was obviously touched by our show of support. He thanked us and immediately we got down to business.

Before the Advisory Committee would meet again the 75th attorney general had resigned and Dick Thornburgh sworn in.

Meese was exonerated by the independent counsel.

SAY SOMETHING FUNNY

On Friday, June 16, 1989, the 93 U.S. attorneys met with President George Bush at the White House. He had invited Attorney General Dick Thornburgh and us for a visit and to hear his remarks relating to law enforcement.

As told elsewhere, President Reagan once had the U.S. attorneys over to the White House; on another occasion he met with us in the Executive Office Building next door. At the latter event wives were guests, so Patti accompanied me.

President Bush spoke for about 15 or 20 minutes with many news cameras rolling. As I recall we were in the East Wing on the second floor of the White House.

In the very early portion of his remarks the president mentioned my name. I was surprised, even startled. (No, I wasn't being fired.) The president referred to my use of humor among my fellow attorneys and Department of Justice personnel. The latter included the attorneys general with whom I had worked, William

French Smith and Ed Meese, as well as then Attorney General Dick Thornburgh.

"Great Scott," I thought; what if the president followed up the reference to my "humor" by suggesting in some fashion that I say something funny. He just might have, you know. The far-fetched thought somehow triggered an idea in my brain: If called on, I could relate my response to a current news event.

The president had just celebrated his 65th birthday and that fact had gotten widespread media attention. I had my spur-of-the-moment answer ready: "In light of your birthday, Mr. President, it's comforting to know that you and I have something very special in common. We're both now on Medicare."

Not necessarily a prize-winning line, but hopefully face-saving if he did call on me. There are probably a jillion really good one-liners I could have used if one had just come to mind. But shock tends to hinder thinking at times like that, especially if you may be called on by the president.

Of course, the president didn't call on me to say something funny and that was just as well. With a campaign for re-election only three years off, he probably wouldn't have found a reference to having qualified for Medicare "something funny."

THE WAY IT IS

In the summer of 1991 I reached age 70. In July of that year I wrote President Bush that I would retire as U.S. Attorney for

North Alabama when my successor had been confirmed by the U.S. Senate and sworn in. Seven months later, March 1992, my replacement, Jack Selden, took office.

For several months prior to leaving office my name was in the local news regularly and prominently. Several times it appeared nationally (<u>Washington Post</u>, <u>New York Times</u>, <u>Time Magazine</u>, for example.)

The news items resulted from the oft-repeated accusation that I was a racist dedicated to getting the Birmingham mayor out of office through a criminal prosecution. It was reported that my desire was to see the mayor removed because he was a minority office holder.

Local papers and radio and television stations gave substantial coverage related to the subject in 1990, the latter part of 1991, early 1992, and again in November 1992 when my successor dumped the matter.

One of the news stories revealed that an Atlanta architect had stated under oath in federal court in Birmingham that he had paid the Birmingham mayor $5,000 in order to get city business.

The architect was convicted and placed on probation, the mayor never even indicted. My successor announced November 12, 1992, that he had declined prosecution.

I was surprised by the no-prosecution decision. I had believed that an indictment was forthcoming. The decision upset a large number of people in law enforcement. (That's putting it mildly. I was out of office, but word gets around.)

I had been impressed with the architect, believing he had veracity. Others possessed a similar belief, including (according to a locally published news story) the federal judge who sentenced the architect.

It can easily be asserted that the architect's allegation that he paid the mayor was itself sufficient to furnish probable cause to support an indictment. (However, to find a defendant guilty beyond a reasonable doubt, a jury would expect such an allegation to be corroborated.)

The day after prosecution was declined, The Birmingham News quoted me, "What objective, what purpose is there (for me) to be bigoted toward the mayor?" I explained that had the mayor been prosecuted and convicted "he would be replaced by (another) minority" (person).

I was asked how I thought I might be remembered concerning this matter. My reported response: "There is no question that politically correct historians will try to make it appear there was validity to those outrageously false allegations that the U.S. attorney had a vendetta against the mayor, that he (the U.S. attorney) was bigoted."

Therefore it was very apropos for U.S. Attorney Jack Selden to include in the same press release in which he stated there would be no prosecution that his review of the history of the investigation convinced him that the matter had been conducted "like any other investigation and handled properly throughout." Of course, it had.

The Birmingham Post-Herald reported February 13, 1992, that the mayor had asked the Office of Professional Responsibility, Department of Justice, to investigate his claims that I was "targeting the mayor because he is black." The request had been made several months earlier. The item declared the DOJ "yesterday officially cleared U.S. Attorney Frank Donaldson of any improprieties in his corruption probe of City Hall."

A local paper correctly reported that I had indicated selective prosecution in my office was unrealistic because 3,500 pending cases demanded attention.

I think also that a variety of checks and balances prevents any federal prosecutor from engaging in a racial vendetta.

A criminal defense attorney's absurd statement that "a prosecutor can indict a ham sandwich" is outrageously flawed.

Look at the barriers:

-The U.S. attorney is appointed by the president and confirmed by the Senate after a full-field FBI background check, so that it is not likely a bigot will become the chief federal prosecutor in any of the 94 federal districts.

-A federal grand jury is made of up 23 persons (of all races); 16 make a quorum; 12 yes votes are needed for a true bill (indictment).

-No prosecutor, witness or judge is in the room with the jurors when they vote whether to indict.

-A judge supervises the grand jury and will hear any of its complaints.

-The U.S. attorney has assistants who are lawyers; men and women, black and white. They are alert to any office shenanigans and are not about to sit tight regarding racist activities.

-Allegations of wrongful conduct made against a prosecutor are reportable to the Office of Professional Responsibility in Main Justice, Washington. OPR investigates such charges, which if supported would result in the prosecutor's removal from office.

-The U.S. attorney has no investigators in his office. The Alabama attorney general has an investigations division. The U.S. attorney does not. The federal prosecutor depends upon appropriate federal agencies for the unearthing and development of facts relating to criminal wrongdoing.

-All agencies have men and women investigative agents of various races. They gather facts and furnish them to the prosecutor. Agents work cooperatively, so they would know if a prosecutor was using them or attempting to do so to pursue a racial objective. They wouldn't put up with it for 15 minutes, and a complaint could be filed with the U.S. attorney general.

-Before a prosecutor obtains an indictment against a public official, the Criminal Division of Main Justice must sign off on an approval — not a formality. Any allegation of impropriety would be closely scrutinized. [3]

---

[3] Some readers may deem the foregoing remarks to be overkill in defense of the U.S. Attorney. Not so. They are in no way intended defensive; rather, they are simply explanatory as non-lawyers have very little understanding of federal criminal procedure.

I have been asked why I didn't get an indictment against the mayor prior to my leaving office in early March 1992. I as much as answered that question several times in speeches that were unrelated to any specific investigation: I said my office took pride in not seeking an indictment until we were ready (or practically ready) for trial. On this point, one will note that some eight months passed after I left office before U.S. Attorney Selden made his decision not to seek an indictment. Thus, one can take for granted the investigation continued for months after I had left office.

I have been asked also why Selden declined to prosecute. I don't know. Of course, he had prosecutorial discretion whether to go forward, as the prosecutor has in every pending matter. Be that as it may, I considered his negative treatment of the matter unfortunate. I thought the people of Birmingham deserved to have the facts aired in court.

By the way, in view of the bogus allegations made against me as U.S. attorney, I probably should mention that a much different view was held by the U.S. attorney general. During my approximately 11 years in office I became the seventh U.S. attorney to receive the attorney general's Flag of Excellence, given for outstanding performance. That hardly was presented in recognition of racism.

The magnificent flag (4'3" x 5'7") is attached to a 10-foot pole, topped by a sparkling golden eagle. The words UNITED STATES ATTORNEY, QUI PRO DOMINA JUSTITIA

SEQUITUR translated: "He who pursues (justice) on behalf of Lady Justice" are emblazoned on the flag.

After I shortened the pole by a foot, the eagle is only two inches from the ceiling in my downstairs den.

United States Attorney – February 27, 1992

United States Attorneys with Attorney General Edwin Meese
1985, Quantico, Virginia
Meese is on the front row, fifth from the left. Frank is to his left.

OTHER PUBLIC SERVICE

*For law professors and practitioners,
service is the name of the game.*

THE BAR EXAMINER

Applicants sitting for the Alabama State Bar Exam had just completed my portion of the test when one of them, an older-than-average law school graduate, approached me. He was upset about something obviously important. I soon learned his concern. He berated me in clear terms for being so "thoughtless and inconsiderate" that I would give "a horrendous exam that no one can be expected to pass."

Understanding that at the end of a long day of tests the examinee was fatigued and that after relaxing a day or two he would think no more about it, I responded, "Perhaps the result won't turn out badly."

I can't say that he was placated, but he quietly walked out of the room, looking down, and shaking his head.

A few months later I saw the former applicant shortly after he was sworn in as an attorney. He was smiling and he spoke to me, authoritatively but pleasantly, "Professor, keep those tough exams going. We lawyers don't need a lot more competition."

I would think that during my nine years as a bar examiner (1965-74) a great many applicants left my part of the tests a bit frustrated only to learn a couple of months later that they had been successful.

Just before I went on the state bar's examining board, there were only three test-givers. There had been only three for many years. Then in 1965 three of us were added. Each was required to test on three subjects.

Additional board members were needed for two reasons: First, an increase in the number of applicants; this was tied to the new requirement that University of Alabama law graduates sit for the exam. Prior to that time UA law grads had "diploma privileges." They did not have to take further tests; for them, graduation was the equivalent of bar admission.

That all now must sit for the exam and pass it to be eligible to practice in the state resulted from the Cumberland School of Law moving from Lebanon, Tennessee, to Birmingham's Howard College in 1961. Its graduates did not have the "diploma privileges."

So, beginning in 1965 all law school graduates who wanted to practice in Alabama had to pass the Alabama bar exam—with one exception: A full-time law professor who taught at

Cumberland or UA for three years and had passed a bar test in another state could be exempted upon application for admission.

There is a bit of irony in that other UA Law School graduates and I who were examiners in 1965 never took a bar exam in this state. We all had been exempted.

When I began my duties, each examiner initially was assigned three subjects. I examined on constitutional law, corporations and equity. Equity was short-lived as more examiners were soon added, so that my subjects were reduced to two.

The number of applicants had mushroomed from a relatively small group in 1965 to several hundred when I resigned from the board in 1974.

In the early 1970s law school enrollment soared nationally. Bar examiners everywhere had more grading to do than ever before.

I well recall spending all of August, after a July bar exam, grading 1,000 essay answers. In September I began wearing glasses while reading. Fortunately, as the number of test-takers grew, the number of examiners grew. Before long, I no longer graded two subjects but continued testing on constitutional law.

Shortly prior to my leaving the board, even constitutional law got two graders, so that as an examiner previously giving two questions, I now had to write only one question and grade those answers, a really big help.

During my stint as an examiner, I plowed new ground, although I had misgivings about it. I thought it wise to see just how ready applicants were to represent clients. Could they put into the real world of law practice what they had learned in law school? To find out I prepared an exam problem that gave the applicants an opportunity to show how prepared they were for a real client, not the make-believe client of a law school classroom.

For example, on one corporation law test I prepared a set of facts that a businessman (the client) took to his lawyer (the applicant) and asked that a corporate charter be drafted. Some applicants had never seen one; that was apparent. Others fumbled with it about as expected, but as I hoped, successfully. However, several charters that were drafted indicated that some test-takers were not uncomfortable at all with this kind of real life law practice.

Twenty-six states were joined by Alabama in the summer of 2003 with a multi-state practice exam. The practice part of the exam in all 27 states is more extensive than anything I ever did, although my experiment was planned with the same objective; not only to determine how well the would-be lawyer had learned certain law, but also to see how practical that person was in addressing a simulated life situation.

I never received any comments on my rudimentary endeavors in this area; I wish that I had gotten feedback, good or bad.

I had gone on the board initially with a University of Alabama law professor and a private practitioner. The examiners agreed early on that a law professor could not examine on any subject he had taught. No doubt that was a good idea lest an applicant get an advantage from a question posed by a former teacher.

In 1974 the suggestion was made and accepted that the wisest approach was for no professor to examine. I came off the board pronto, although disagreeing with the idea, for no one is better qualified to write law exam questions and grade essay answers than professionals who write questions and grade answers all the time.

However, I was ready to be done with the chore. The stipend was de minimis; the eyestrain was not. Law school exam grading in June, followed by bar exam grading in August was a bit much. Besides, August was my family vacation time.

SUPREME COURT ASSIGNMENT

From 1819, the year Alabama was admitted to the Union, until 1973, trial lawyers practicing in Alabama state courts used two separate systems of pleading and procedure in non-criminal cases. Modified common law pleading as done under the common law of England, with some state statutory changes, was the system used in our civil law courts. However, in Alabama equity courts, equity pleading was required under a substantially different set of rules.

Lawyers who engaged in general trial work, and that was most attorneys in the old days, had to learn two sets of rules, one for state civil law and one for equity practice.

The federal courts followed state pleading rules for more than 100 years so that during that time Alabama lawyers did not have to master a third set of rules. But in 1938 the U.S Supreme Court adopted rules of civil procedure for lawyers practicing in the U.S. district courts; thereafter, Alabama lawyers who tried civil law cases in both state and federal courts had to know three sets of rules: for federal court, state civil court, and state equity court.

In 1971 a big change got under way. Immediately following legislation that gave the Alabama Supreme Court rule-making power, Chief Justice Howell Heflin and his court colleagues wasted no time pursuing action under the new legislation. A 15-member Civil Rules Advisory Committee was named to draft a set of civil procedure rules for Alabama lawyers.

The committee was comprised of two state trial court judges, two law professors, and 11 practitioners, two of whom were state legislators.

The legislature made possible the promulgation of one pleading and procedure system, rather than two, thus providing for the merger of law and equity under one set of rules for Alabama state law practice.

1972 Civil Rules Committee
Frank seated third from left (back row)

The Alabama Supreme Court, on the recommendation of my boss, Cumberland Law School Dean Arthur A. Weeks, named me as a member of the committee (one of the two law professors).

Without doubt, from the time of the committee's first meeting until the rules were drafted and adopted by the court, the members knew they were in a history making position. We tackled our assignment with enthusiasm; all agreed that law and equity should be merged. Believing wholeheartedly in the project, we developed a splendid camaraderie. Our drafting work was completed within a year.

The Alabama Supreme Court adopted the rules our committee had submitted to it with minor modification and made them effective for Alabama lawyers on July 3, 1973.

Of course, this meant that attorneys handling civil cases in Alabama state courts had to learn a brand new set of rules. That was a cinch for those few lawyers who had a substantial federal practice; for the state's new rules were very similar to the federal rules.

Most lawyers needed study.• For the bar members to get a jump on understanding the new rules and to get their acceptance off to a good start, several committee members were asked to conduct classes for lawyers and judges prior to the effective date of the rules. Classes were held in Huntsville, Birmingham, Montgomery, and Mobile.

I taught an hour and a half class in each city. Attendance averaged 300 per class session. I found a pleasant difference in the attorneys' keen interest in the new rules rather than the lack of interest seven years earlier when several other attorneys and I held classes for lawyers and judges on Alabama's soon to be effective new Uniform Commercial Code. At that time we had averaged 25 lawyers at each class in the same four sites.

Although our Civil Rules Committee members served without pay, those of us who conducted classes received a modest stipend for each session. I emphasize modest. Skimpy would be more accurate. But I complain not.

Many lawyers contribute time and talent for betterment of the profession. I emphasized to many of my law students that there are substantial non-monetary rewards for service. After all, in the legal profession service is the name of the game. Usually, but not always, the service is to the lawyer's clients.

TV STAR

The year after I left the U.S. Attorney's Office in 1992 a Birmingham television station, Channel 42, the CBS outlet in Birmingham, invited me to be a contributing editor for a new segment to be part of the 6 p.m. newscast.

The management wrote me, "We call it 'Parting Shot'...contributing editors to 'Parting Shot' will be asked to write on issues that concern them...The segments will be taped in the station's studios and shown at about 6:27 p.m. on Monday, Wednesday, and Friday evenings."

I was told that each segment would run about two minutes and that a maximum of two per month could be expected.

No presentation was to be remunerated monetarily. Of course not. But sounding off publicly on topics of one's particular interest has some non-depositable rewards.

My first "Parting Shot" episode was shown in May 1993: "Change the Campaign Law for Judges?" Judicial campaigns in Alabama had not been going too well, hence my selection of that topic. There was a move underway for these judges to be selected by a few "hand-picked" political partisans.

Though I felt like I was a voice "crying in the wilderness" of a smelly political arena, I felt it necessary to speak out against that change.

Fortunately, 17 years later state court judges are still chosen by the electorate, not at all because I had addressed the subject. In any event, sounding off on the subject, and others, may have had a therapeutic effect on the TV star.

Many topics (mine and those of other contributing editors) frequently dealt with controversial subjects. I was pleased that the station manager never put a damper on any issue on which I spoke.

Some issues were ahead of their time. For example, I think of the need we have in this state for a new constitution. Recently there has been a move afoot for one, but our political leaders do not seem sufficiently interested.

I pointed out in a "Parting Shot" which aired on November 30, 1993, that the Alabama Constitution had been adopted in 1901 and had been amended more than 550 times. The TV spot generated no interest of consequence, although I had mentioned in the film that the present Constitution had been amended an average of six times a year for 92 years.

If one desired to move a copy of the 1901 Constitution and its amendments from one site to another, a wheelbarrow would be needed.

When "Parting Shot" filming began, I had recently completed nearly 11 years in law enforcement as a federal prosecutor. However, my favorite subject for the program was not law enforcement but was education. I thoroughly enjoyed writing about it.

My first "Parting Shot" on the subject was "Teach Kids to Read." But as things turned out, my favorite of favorites, "Teach Kids to Read the Funnies," written in August 1995 never filmed. I don't recall why, perhaps because the "Parting Shot" segment was terminated just before the topic was to be filmed.

I had written in part, "The cartoon pages of newspapers should be required reading in all grade schools. That's right — the funny papers ought to be must reading for school kids."

I wish the topic had been filmed and shown. Not that it was an earth-shaker, but simply because I liked it. And the subject has merit.

During the approximately two and a half years the program aired, I did only 24 of the two-minute presentations. I could have done more had I made the effort. I wish that I had done so. The presentations were fun.

LAW SCHOOL ATTACHMENT

In addition to dedicating myself to good teaching for 43 years in the Cumberland School of Law, I will comment on three other contributions to the school.

The first one I'll mention was the last to take place, occurring mostly in the 1980s. During my service as U.S. Attorney (1981-92) I hired 28 assistant U.S. attorneys, 25 of them

Cumberland graduates and members of the Alabama Bar Association.

Only one of the 28 disappointed me. At the time he was employed, I was convinced he possessed the personal qualities I liked and needed in the office; early on, his job performance revealed that a scholar he was not. Simply put, the poor guy was out of his league. He was clearly deficient in the legal skills the position required, so much so that I asked myself how I had decided to bring him on board. Well, slip-ups happen.

There were and are several stars among the others. Several continue their work as lawyers in the U.S. attorney's office. I get good reports, unofficially, of course.

When I retired from the office in March 1992, I had employed more Cumberland graduates than any other law firm ever. Whether that record stands after 18-plus years, I don't know, but it probably does. However, I would be pleased to learn that another group of lawyers had demonstrated their confidence in Cumberland graduates by hiring more than I did.

As U.S. attorney I had one big advantage in the hiring process — the opportunity to observe in the classroom most of those I hired.

Nineteen years as a Cumberland law professor preceded my federal position. Thereafter it was my good fortune to teach a course one evening a week during my 11-year tenure as U.S. Attorney. Thus, several of my A students found their way into my office as assistant U.S. attorneys.

My "first assistant" (top ranking among the assistants), Leon "Buddy" Kelly, was the first person I hired. He had graduated with the top academic record among the 214 graduates, class of 1977. Buddy had been enrolled in a couple of my classes.

My second contribution began on November 1, 1979, with the establishment of the Professor Frank Donaldson Civil Procedure Writing Award. This monetary award is a single "prize," winner take all (no second and third place awards) for the best paper on any civil procedure topic, preferably of national interest.

The contest rules began with a $100 award. The winner for 2000 received $750. The latest award is established for $1,000.

I hope that soon the amount will exceed $1,000 and that it will continue to increase, even substantially. A fond hope is that a Cumberland graduate or enough alumni will contribute sufficiently to the award to make it self-funding through earned interest to produce at least $1,000.

An initial gift of $40,000 would keep the award in perpetuity. I have thought of continuing to fund the contest, assuring its survival now that I have retired, but I believe that one or more alumni should be given the opportunity to do so. From my contributions and the interest therefrom, the Samford University endowment fund has on hand, as of this writing, more than $3,000 for the civil procedures writing contest.

The third contribution has nothing to do with money. Actually it was a joint project with George P. Ford, Jr., one of my students.

In 1970 Dean Arthur Weeks and I, as associate dean, looked into qualifying Cumberland for Order of the Coif. The Coif is conferred upon those students who have outstanding law school academic records. A recipient of the award must have enrolled in a law school authorized to make the Coif awards.

Our effort didn't pan out because at the time our application was premature; the law school needed growth in a couple of areas, despite much progress made since arriving at Samford (then Howard College) less than a decade before.

As none of our top students were to receive the Coif award, George Ford and I decided, with dean and faculty approval, to create an opportunity for the students to receive an honor more difficult to obtain than the Coif. We named the prestigious honor Curia Honoris, to be the legal honor society of the Cumberland School of Law of Samford University.

Selection to Curia Honoris is among the law school's highest distinctions. Each spring the faculty chooses a small number of graduates from the previous year, each of whom was graduated in the top 10 percent of his or her class with a cumulative grade point average of 3.0 or higher (4-point scale), and each would have contributed to the law school through extra-curricular activities.

The dean and faculty adopted the constitution for Curia Honoris in November 1972. Shortly thereafter we selected graduates from the classes of 1966 through 1972 for the first induction, which took place on an April morning in 1973.

Each spring since, the law school has hosted an investiture ceremony at an Awards Day program.

Of course, George Ford was among the first Curia Honoris inductees. One of his several qualifications for the honor was his contribution to the law school in helping create the honor society.

Epilogue: I was informed in 1972 that George Ford's score on the Alabama state bar exam was the highest recorded. A quarter-century later George became a Fellow of the American College of Trial Lawyers. To my surprise? No way.

KEEPSAKES FOR SERVICE

For as long as I can remember I've enjoyed giving speeches. And, for the most part, "giving" is the correct term, not overworked in this case.

Among the hundreds of times I've spoken and to a wide variety of audiences (church, civic, social, educational, political, legal, etc.) most friendly but not all, only a handful have presented me with honorariums or paid fees. Several times I have declined payment. As U.S. attorney, very early on I determined to decline any offer of money, any amount, even if a token sum or for travel expenses.

Once, however, I yearned to be rewarded with a physical token of thanks after a particular talk. A Samford University home economics professor invited me, as a university colleague, to address her students, all female, on the subject of domestic relations. Although we offered a domestic relations course in the law school, I had never taught it. But, in my law practice I had represented clients in divorce proceedings and clients who had various domestic relations problems. So, I happily accepted her invitation to address her students on a certain day at 11 a.m.

We met in a room next to the kitchen, where from the wonderful aroma it was apparent the students were brewing a pot of vegetable soup.

As I talked the smell became more and more appealing, until by the time my remarks ended I had whetted an appetite that would make it easy to devour not one, but two bowls of their delicious offering — my idea of a sumptuous honorarium!

At the conclusion of the class session the home economics professor and the students were very courteous, saying, "Thanks, thanks very much," as they politely ushered me, soupless, from the room.

Sometime later it occurred to me that I might be asked again to speak to the professor's 11 a.m. class, and, if so, I decided I would inquire, "What will you and your students be serving us for lunch?" The opportunity to pose the question to her never arose. There was not another invitation.

Accepting token tangible gifts, however, was not taboo. The result has been an interesting array of coffee mugs galore, pencils, writing pens, rulers, letter-openers, umbrellas, paperweights, key chains, and the like. Most of these came from civic clubs, to whom I made most of the 375 speeches during my 11 years as U.S. attorney. But almost all the gift presenters sabotaged me. How? Several times I've wanted to pass some of the gifts to someone else as a token of my thanks for a person's act of thoughtfulness. But I couldn't, and here's why: the gift-giving organization had its name printed, stamped or engraved on its gift.

For example, a writing pen in a neat little box (worth $10 at most) had the club's name on the pen. That makes it a real keepsake!

My wife wishes I would use the pens and dispose of them. But what about all the coffee mugs, and the various other items? Well, one simple solution comes to mind: My estate! Why not leave their disposal to someone else? Is that buck passing? Perhaps, but it avoids current hassles and solves the problem for now. No need to sweat over minutiae.

30th Anniversary Reunion
Alabama Civil Rules Committee, 2003
Judicial Building, Montgomery, Alabama
Left to right: Frank Donaldson, Mayer W. Perloff, Oakley Melton, Alabama
Supreme Court Justice Champ Lyons, U. S. District Court Judge Foy Guin,
James Klinefelter, Jack Livingston.

FINAL MILITARY DUTY

*Sometimes, upon the urging of others, we prioritize our
activities in a way different from what we would have
done if left to our own choices.*

AIR FORCE RESERVIST

In the fall after August graduation from the University of
Alabama Law School and soon after opening my law office
(Donaldson & Thompson) on October 1, 1954, I applied to become
active as an Air Force Reservist in Birmingham.

I had been discharged as a captain from the U.S. Army Air
Forces in January 1946, and thereafter had flown as a pilot in the
reserves.

My last flight as a reservist had been in a T6, on June 27,
1947, at the Marietta, Georgia, air base. That was about three
weeks before I joined the FBI as an agent at the bureau's academy
in Quantico, Virginia.

As events developed, the last time I piloted a military aircraft was that late June day at Marietta.

Not long after FBI Director Hoover sent me to Washington State in October 1947, I discussed with a military officer in Spokane my interest in resuming reserve activity. My service then would have been for the first time with the U.S. Air Force, not the Army Air Forces, because in July 1947, Congress, by statute, made the U.S. Air Force a separate military department. Army Air Forces pilot records became those of the U.S. Air Force.

The officer in Spokane and I could not work out certain details, so I became a non-affiliated reservist for about seven years. That was just as well because the FBI work and later law school demands left little time for military responsibilities.

But in the fall of 1954, I decided that my work schedule and my family obligations would not preclude reservist duties one evening a month and 15 days active duty each summer. My law partner, William A. Thompson, was active in the Army Reserve and had similar requirements.

The Birmingham Air Reserve Center, situated downtown in the Calder Building, was convenient to both home and office.

I became acquainted there with, among others, Birmingham lawyers Larry Kloess, Wilbur Silberman, James Bradford, and Tuscaloosa attorney James Buck. Kloess, Buck and I served two summer tours together and became close friends.

I had hoped that reserve duty might open the door for me to fly locally, but that didn't happen. At the time there was no reserve flight unit in Birmingham, so in effect I was grounded, although my primary military classification was "pilot, fighter."

Any flying would be limited to the short-term summer tour of duty or travel to an inconvenient Air Force base.

In the summer of 1955 I pulled 15 days active duty at Maxwell Air Force Base, Montgomery. I did only two more summer tours: 1956 at Robins Air Force Base and the following year at Turner Air Force Base, both in Georgia.

Patti put her foot down against my flying jets — well, on my flying anything, but especially jets. Her reasoning was sound: I flew propeller planes in the war, not jets. I was older, my reflexes were slower and the planes faster. That didn't come out on the plus side.

The commercial license and instrument rating I'd gotten in 1945 during the war, looking toward possible civilian use, had long expired, so giving up flying altogether seemed inevitable. I liked flying immensely. I never performed any task I enjoyed more, but now I threw in the towel without verbal complaint. The time comes when some things must be left behind.

So in 1955, after the Maxwell tour, I switched my primary military occupational specialty (MOS) from pilot (MOS 112E) to legal officer (MOS 882) and served my remaining reserve duties with the Judge Advocate General's Department. That included legal work at Robins and Turner Air Force bases during my summer tours. Coinciding with my change in the MOS came a promotion in 1956 to major.

In the fall of 1957 the Air Force made clear that the regular officers were not fond of reservists, indicating a plain disinterest in us. Coupling that with our two young sons' need for more of my attention, I decided to chunk the reserves. In early 1958 I resigned, leaving for keeps my affiliated activity with the military.

The Air Force finally responded to my resignation. I was honorably discharged on September 13, 1962. I had been sworn in as a private on May 13, 1942; commissioned December 13, 1942, and mustered out on September 13, 1962.

I had hoped that one of our sons would attend the Air Force Academy and become a pilot, but neither ever showed the slightest interest. Perhaps I made a mistake in the 1960s when Steve and David were teenagers, telling them, "If I were 19 or 20 years of age and there was any way to get an appointment to the Air Force Academy, I would be a cadet there in a flash."

Perhaps it was just as well they turned down, out of hand, their father's push. Had they not done so, I'm sure their mother's beautiful blond hair would have become prematurely gray, especially with the Vietnam fiasco in full sway.

THE OLD AND THE BOLD

Sometime during the summer of 1955 I served 15 days active duty in the Air Force Reserve in pilot status at Maxwell Air Force Base, but I did no flying, for two reasons. First, only a few days prior to the date of the new tour of duty to begin I had surgery on the calf of my left leg to remove a neuroma, and for three or four days I was on crutches; for the remainder of the tour I limped a bit.

So, no flying, and because of this circumstance the high brass in the unit at Maxwell didn't know what to do with me, unusual for the military. For 15 days I just hung around, probably a general nuisance.

The second reason I did no flying (and I might have squeezed some in the last few days of the tour, particularly as a co-pilot or as a passenger) was the result of a promise my wife extracted from me. Just before I had left home, she had pleaded with me to promise I wouldn't leave the ground. Her pitch was she didn't want me taking any chances that might prevent my helping her rear our two sons, a 1-year-old and a 3-year-old.

In fact, Patti insisted I give up flying altogether. So I did give it up, and thereafter served in the reserve as a lawyer. That meant that I had changed my military occupational specialty from pilot to legal; that my foremost love had terminated my lifelong love. No other person will ever know the joy I had experienced as a pilot. No question, had I been a bachelor, I would have pursued flying to the end. But, then, as a really bold pilot handling Air Force fighter planes, I probably would not have become an "old" bachelor.

I think of a favorite aphorism I heard during WWII:

> *There are old pilots.   There are bold pilots.*
> *But very few old, bold pilots.*

Donaldson with cadet name tag
Aviation Cadet Class 42-X Reunion
San Antonio, Texas - 1992

COURAGE, QUESTIONS, AND WONDER

For those of us who like to think, there is a great deal in life to ponder... and ponder some more.

LOOKING FOR A TWIN

Many people have done something no one else has done. A few notable examples: The Wright Brothers were first to fly a plane. Alan Shepard was first in outer space. John Glenn was the first American to orbit the earth. Neil Armstrong and Buzz Aldrin were the first to walk on the moon.

These are internationally recognized achievements. But we all are aware of less-recognized but still worthy achievements, some of which occur close to home, even at home.

Law Professor Albert Brewer was speaker of the Alabama House of Representatives, then Lieutenant Governor and Governor. Jeff Sessions was United States Attorney, Alabama Attorney General, and is a U.S. Senator. Patti Donaldson makes the world's best vegetable soup and prune cake.

Because people all around us achieve and succeed, I was not surprised when asked, "Can you, Frank Donaldson, claim to have done anything unique, something no one else has done?"

I responded not in boast, but in curiosity.

I wonder if anyone else, anywhere "out there," was a pilot in World War II, has been an FBI agent, a practicing lawyer, a law professor (40-plus years), U.S. Attorney (11 years), a Sunday school teacher for more than 5 decades, and has had the same spouse for 3 score years. If anyone has experienced all these, please give me a call or drop me a note—we have a lot in common!

GETTING THE BOOT — TWICE!

Twice in my life I have been fired from a job. The first time was in 1945 during WWII when I was the operations officer at Aloe Field near Victoria, Texas. I'm not sure how a dispute with my superior arose, but because he was aggravated with me he saw that my assistant, a captain, was made operations officer and I was demoted to assistant operations officer.

I learned that my new boss, my former assistant, was, if not an outright screwball, to say it kindly, a peculiar, strange duck. So, after the switch it suited me fine for him to do his thing and for me to do mine.

I brought all of this on myself. One word describes it: arrogance. As the matter involved a superior officer, "insolence" also is not inappropriate.

As the operations officer, I was thoroughly filled with hubris. After all, I knew the job well, handled my personnel satisfactorily, and got the work assigned to me done efficiently and consistently. But when my superior officer ordered me to make a certain change (details of which I don't recall), I considered his order a suggestion and argued with him about it in a very stubborn manner — and got what I deserved: booted.

The second time I was booted was 13 years later at Howard College while employed as an instructor. For three years I had taught a course in the evening division in the undergraduate school (there was no law school at Howard at the time).

During the summer of 1957 Howard moved from the East Lake area in Birmingham to its new campus on 400 beautiful, wooded acres in Homewood, some six miles from the old location.

The 1957-58 academic year's spring term ended in May 1958, which closed out the first full year of studies on the new campus.

The course I taught that spring had enrolled about 60 students and the term was scheduled to go further into May than I had anticipated. I was anxious to take Patti, Steve, 6, and David, 4, to the beach at Panama City, Florida. Thus, eager to leave on our trip, I gave the exam early, with nary a word to the dean about it.

The dean took exception — he didn't like his team member's breach one whit. Again, on my part, arrogance. Doing my own thing, my way. Once again I was booted. For the record: I was invited back to Howard College in 1962, that time as a law professor.

Of course, I trust there won't be a third firing — and if there is, I like to think it won't be because of arrogance. And yet, and yet…in one sense arrogance is not so bad as a ground for firing, especially as contrasted with, say, senility. Arrogance, however, can be avoided and I don't suppose the same can be said of senility. The solution then is not to be arrogant and to retire when it's time. I hope to remember that!

GUARDIAN ANGEL?

Many times in my life I have been convinced beyond any doubt God had conferred upon me special protection from danger. I'm equally convinced that God conferred the protection even when I was unaware of impending peril.

When I was young and given uncommon protection I seldom ever thought of a guardian angel. After all, protection from harm was bestowed as a special gift from God. But why this care? And why me? I don't know, but I know that it began during my boyhood.

In my early teens I built a "chinning bar" in our yard. The bar was about eight feet off the ground. One end of a 5-foot, ¾ inch pipe was fastened to the top of a post, the other end fastened to a huge oak tree.

I used the bar mainly to do chin-ups. Sometimes I engaged in other exercises on the bar. Once while exercising I flipped off the top and fell to the hard ground on my back. I recall that every part of my back and head hit the ground simultaneously. I could not have been more horizontal; my weight was evenly distributed from head to toe.

The fall left me momentarily dazed, but I shortly walked away without injury.

Although my own mistake brought the fall, a Guiding Hand protected me against broken bones or worse. I later thought, "Suppose a stool that I sometimes used to reach the bar had been left directly under me. Suppose the ground had not been level. Or suppose I had fallen awkwardly with most of my weight on one side. Or I had landed headfirst." Any one or a combination of positions could have resulted in a broken neck or other serious injury.

Many people have had close calls traveling the Florida Short Route. I'm one of them. I hitchhiked several times to and fro between my home in Phenix City and Howard College in Birmingham.

On one occasion en route home I rode alone in the back seat of a four-door sedan. Two mature, executive-type adult males were up front. The one behind the wheel had a heavy foot on the accelerator. As we topped a ridge an oncoming auto, attempting to pass another car, was speeding toward us, almost upon us, on our side of the highway. My driver suddenly jerked his steering wheel to the right, sending our vehicle off the road onto the shoulder. He never touched the brakes; instead he floor-boarded the accelerator.

In what seemed like a split second we had left the shoulder and were safely back on the highway in our lane.

The driver's skill, his quick reflexes, a lengthy grassy shoulder, sufficiently level, provided for the safety of the three of us.

A few years later I was an instructor pilot in the Army Air Forces. On March 8, 1943, while we were flying over Kansas wheat fields, my plane collided in mid-air with a cadet's plane. We had been having fun pretending we were in a "dogfight" when our planes hit, slicing off part of a wing on each of the planes. A few feet had separated us from oblivion. We were able to fly safely back to our base at Strother Field (between Winfield and Arkansas City, Kansas). Of course I was chewed out for engaging in mock dogfighting with a cadet, although I was not aware of a specific prohibition of such antics.

On that occasion the Heavenly Guiding Hand protected this 21-year-old second lieutenant, my passenger (a sergeant along for a joyride), and the cadet.

In my flying career I also had three deadstick landings without incident. One such landing occurred when the engine on my P-47 quit while I was flying over the Texas Panhandle. The other two forced landings happened in training planes. All were engine failures and all were in daytime. I flew each undamaged airplane away from where I had landed it.

Several years later I was an FBI agent assigned to the Birmingham office. One afternoon a few miles north of suburban Tarrant another motorist ran me off the road. I was headed south, the other driver north. As we rounded a curve, he came over the center line onto my side of the road. To avoid a head-on collision, I had to veer quickly onto the side of the road. Fortunately there were no obstructions and I brought my car to a safe stop.

I stopped only momentarily. The other vehicle never slowed, so I turned around and pursued it. Catching up, I motioned for the driver to pull over. I walked to the side of the vehicle, keeping my hand on or close to my revolver and remarked about being forced off the road.

The driver was obviously drunk as were his three adult male passengers. I don't think I was then in any danger because none of the four appeared able to stand.

The Lord had doubly blessed me, first, by providing room for me to get off the road; second, by enabling me to stay cool and not shoot out the tires on the drunks' vehicle. The temptation had been strong.

I'm very pleased that I did not use my gun then, or ever. God's protection was there during my five years as an FBI agent, for I was never wounded, not even shot at or was otherwise attacked. Neither did I shoot, attack, or wound anyone.

I could relate a number of close calls, all without injury.

I remember my Helena pastor, the Reverend Pat Minshew, in a public prayer thanking God for "protection from unseen danger."

Has protection been granted me from imminent danger that I was unaware of? I have no doubt that my close calls with potential peril greatly outnumber those of which I was aware.

So...a Guardian Angel? Whether yes or no, the Lord's protective care has been bestowed upon this grateful recipient.

COLLEGE DAYS AND THESE DAYS

During the summer of 1939, at age 17, after graduation from high school, I did manual labor on the campus of Southern Union Junior College, Wadley, Alabama.

The college had a couple of milk cows, a vegetable garden and wood was burned in a big outdoor furnace used to heat the men's dormitory on cold days. All of this required substantial labor, most of it coming from students.

The following summer I worked on the campus of Howard College in Birmingham, again doing physical labor, but doubling my earnings.

The summer after my sophomore year was a different story. I worked at the suburban Wenonah iron ore plant, part of U.S. Steel, near Birmingham.

A Howard classmate, Wheeler Flemming, had told me about Wenonah, where he had just gone to work. I rode in Wheeler's car to and from the Lambda Chi Alpha house, where I lived most of the summer of 1941. Mama moved from Phenix City to Birmingham the same summer, so I left the fraternity house in late July or early August and moved into her home across the street from Howard.

The two pre-war summers at Howard were rewarding. One reason was I built up a lot of endurance. At the Wenonah plant my main job was shoveling iron ore, some days for eight hours, longer if there was overtime. I don't believe anyone working in my area handled more ore than I did, nor did anyone work when I took time out to rest.

In the evenings after work I was the typical college boy of those years with bundles of energy and endurance. Back then I was 5 feet 7 ½ inches and weighed 135 pounds. Two years later I had gained an inch in height. Nearly 70 years later the endurance figure has changed significantly.

Today I do not labor by the hour for money or for credit with a bursar. My income for more than half a century has come from non-manual labor; my energy continues to be unusually abundant, but my endurance is another story.

All of the foregoing came to mind recently while I was doing physical labor in my yard. I had worked in the yard an hour and a half before breakfast. By the time I stopped work at 8 a.m. the temperature was about 80 degrees and I was ready to quit for the day.

I also walk briskly five or six times a week for about 40 minutes per walk. Two mornings last week I walked 23 minutes and quit. The air was very muggy and the temperature more than 80 degrees each of the two mornings and the heat index several points higher.

Long ago during those college summers the sun was just as hot, but the heat didn't hinder my job performance for a full day's work. Back then I usually worked in short-sleeve cotton shirts and wore easily washable cotton trousers. Wearing an undershirt was unheard of. A "heat index" was also unheard of and had there been one, it wouldn't have meant anything. Work, with appropriate endurance, would have gone right on.

So what's the point? It is this: Notwithstanding regular exercise, wholesome food, and what some might call "clean living" (no smoking or drinking), the passing of six decades cuts into one's endurance. Perhaps this is why the Lord left child-rearing to young couples.

When my four children were growing up, Patti and I were blessed with both patience and endurance (perhaps more of the latter than the former). But today, after my small grandchildren visit a few hours, I enjoy hearing, "Bye, bye, Granddaddy."

THE GENEROUS PLAYBOY

The Alabama State Bar Examination is administered in February and July of each year and has been for as long as I can remember.

One day not long after the July bar exam results were furnished to the applicants, a young man knocked on my door at the Cumberland Law School and introduced himself. He was not a Cumberland alumnus but a graduate of a well-recognized law school far from Alabama. He said, "I hope you will help me. I just got the results from the Alabama Bar Exam and I flunked."

He explained that he had done well in law school and had underestimated the difficulty of the Alabama Bar Exam. He told me that he was clearly without excuse for not passing, that upon graduating from law school in May he had vacationed on the Riviera, played, had fun, and not studied. He said he was satisfied with the exam results on all the subjects except Alabama (modified) common law pleading and equity pleading, subjects he had failed.

His visit was to request my suggestions on how to study for these two subjects, and he wanted recommendations for course materials. Although at that time I taught equity pleading and not common law pleading, I gave him suggestions and recommendations for both subjects.

I also suggested he talk with my colleague, Professor Claude Bankester, who taught common law pleading.

Claude was a true scholar. I considered him especially so. He was not only learned in the law, he had his feet planted firmly on solid soil, was full of common sense, unusually winsome and was kind and helpful to students one-on-one in his office.

Claude also possessed a marvelous sense of humor. I well recall him mentioning to me one afternoon, "Would you believe I forgot to go to a class this morning?" Since he seemed quite concerned, I responded, "Think nothing of it, could happen to anyone of us."

"Oh, I know," he replied. "What bothers me is how many classes have I forgotten to attend that I never remembered I forgot?"

I expect the anxious young law graduate talked with Claude. In any event the young man apparently boned up on the two subjects for he was admitted to the Alabama bar the next year.

As a practicing attorney he has become eminently successful.

A QUESTION OF NUMBERS

During the summer of 1953 Educational Director Dennis Cuniff of Calvary Baptist Church in Tuscaloosa asked me to teach an adult men's Sunday school class. I said yes. Then he told me he wanted "us" to organize a class for men ages 30 to 40 starting in September.

I had not taught before but had participated in several Bible study groups. Patti and I were members of Calvary and I had a year left in the University of Alabama Law School.

The class organized well and I taught until September 1954 when Patti and I with our two sons returned to Birmingham, where

I began law practice. A few months later we moved to Helena. In 1956 I began teaching a class in our new church, Helena Baptist. Since then I have taught regularly except for a brief time in 1978 after we moved to Homewood. The first Sunday of October, 1978, our family joined nearby Dawson Memorial Baptist.

The class I now teach is comprised of men and women, ages 55 to 70. And that brings me to the point of these remarks. In my 50 years of Bible teaching I never have had a large class. At Calvary, attendance usually was 12 to 15, at Helena from one or two to a dozen, at Dawson from seven or eight to 20 or 25. Recent attendance has averaged about 10 to 12.

In view of these small attendances, occasionally I pondered: If there is a problem, what is it? I study diligently and present Bible material with a desire to be both interesting and effective.

Are study sessions too long? Seats too hard? Do I have an unrecognized bad habit? Failure to follow up during the week on class members' personal lives?

If during the five decades of Bible teaching I had been a preacher of the Gospel of Jesus Christ and my track record in preaching was equivalent to my record in teaching, my congregations would have been small, perhaps 100 or so, and I might have been urged periodically to preach elsewhere.

Why does the Lord enable some ministers to attract large congregations and others only small ones? Likewise for Sunday school teachers?

Reverend Pat Minshew was our Helena pastor for 14 ½ years of his 50-year ministry. The best Sunday school attendance in the mid-1960s, reflecting the strength of the church, averaged 147. "Brother" Pat, who had a wife and two sons, was paid $100 a week. He and his wife are Christian gems.

When we became members of Dawson in 1978, Sunday school attendance there averaged 2,000. Pastor Edgar Arendall held two morning worship services. I don't know what his salary was, but on his 25th anniversary as pastor there, the church membership gave him and his wife, Sara, a deed to the house where they resided. Upon retirement 11 years later, the church gave him a new car and an extensive trip.

I do not propose to know why one of God's servants was pastor of small churches for 50 years; the other, pastor of a large, ever-expanding church for 36 years.

For 30-plus years our son Steve has taught young adults in Sunday school. More than once he has had a class enrollment of 75. The class was purposely downsized, so that an additional class could be started; soon membership in his class was again 75.

Patti's Sunday school class of elderly women exceeds 40.

Neither do I know why my Sunday school teaching has been limited to small classes. But this I do know: I'm proud of the excellent teaching of Steve and his mother.

By the way, Steve once was a pupil in my class of teenagers.

Recently the members of my Sunday School class at Dawson gave me the book The Journey by Billy Graham. I thanked them, then said with a grin, "One Sunday morning at Christmas I visited Henry Hoffman's class and the members gave him four $50 bills." John Burland, president of the class, blurted out, "But he's a better teacher than you are!"

I responded, "You nailed that one."

TESTIMONIES

Today I turned 80 (September 8, 2001). This morning I played nine holes of golf — walking, not riding in a cart. Some of the 46 strokes were not very good, but as I saw them, I hit a few really neat ones.

On turning 80 I recall, with much fondness, an unusual event. Not on the golf course, but something that occurred one evening a few years ago at the Vestavia Bowling Lanes.

All 28 lanes were occupied with league bowlers when the lanes manager came on the loudspeaker, "Ladies and gentlemen, today is Mr. Wilson Hamilton's 80th birthday. He has asked to speak with you."

Wilson took the microphone, spoke briefly about bowling, then concluded, "Friends, I wish to take this opportunity to publicly thank my Lord and Savior Jesus Christ for giving me these wonderful 80 years."

We were all respectfully quiet while he spoke. Not a pin fell, not a ball rolled. Although we weren't a church-sponsored group of bowlers, there was a brief sense of reverence in the smoke-filled air.

I thought, "What courage! Wilson just couldn't hold back his desire to use the time and place to express his gratitude for a lifetime of blessings."

A short time later I mentioned Wilson's statement to Dr. Mabry Lunceford, retired Samford University religion professor, who responded, "My, my, I wish I had thought to say something like that on my recent 75th birthday."

After 15 consecutive years of league bowling, I rolled my last ball. I finally had had enough of second-hand cigarette smoke. But if I still were in a league, I don't know that on my 80th birthday I would do what Wilson did. However, I am willing to paraphrase him with this prayer: "Thank you, Lord, for giving me these 80 wonderful years."

In the morning I will be neither bowling nor playing golf, but will be back in a Cumberland School of Law classroom. And I will thank God that work is a special joy in this delightful time on earth.

PRIVATE DONALDSON

A friend and I once discussed rewards and rank in Heaven. We agreed that the Bible reveals that we Christians will be rewarded for good deeds on Earth. However, neither of us had Scripture to support our position that there also will be a ranking in

Heaven. We did agree that some of us will be generals and some privates, so to speak, in God's heavenly army of saints.

Our talk clearly indicated what he and I believed: Those on earth who had performed little service were to be privates, whereas those who had rendered much service could expect a generalship.

The very night after the conversation with my friend I had the following dream: I had just entered Heaven and was escorted to St. Peter, who promptly peppered me with questions. He asked my name, age, marital status, children, place from which I'd come, etc. I responded willingly. St. Peter then asked another type question: "What contribution did you make toward a higher quality of life for others?"

My prompt response: "My country, the United States, is very prosperous, and we periodically send food, clothing, medicine and other supplies to needy people on Planet Earth. Sometimes we send money. We've helped like this for years," and as sort of an afterthought, "and I've always paid my taxes."

St. Peter indicated impatience. "You don't seem to understand," he said. He pointed to an area of activity and called out, "Bring a reporter over here." He planned to take my deposition, and that unnerved me. With his first question I saw where he was headed. "Never mind the United States sending aid to other countries," he said. "What did you do?"

He had my full attention as he continued with numerous questions, such as,

"Have you taken food to a hungry neighbor?

Have you invited a beggar at your door to come in for a meal?

Have you visited an inmate in the local jail?

Have you visited patients in hospitals?

Have you sought help for someone ill or injured?

Have you spoon-fed an ill adult, a stranger?

How often have you taken kindling or firewood to an elderly widow on a cold night?"

Suddenly St. Peter changed his line of questioning:

"Were you a friendly, good-natured person?

Were you fair at work? At play?

Were you prejudiced toward a fellow being?

Did you protest a burst of profanity in your presence?

How did you respond when Almighty God's name was taken in vain?"

St. Peter's questions really hit home, especially when he asked, "Did you encourage other Christians? Explain how."

There were yet other questions, and I was uneasy, to say the least. Finally St. Peter gently inquired: "What is your track record in making known your faith in Jesus?"

Immediately after my feeble responses to his many questions, a transcript of my replies was handed to St. Peter. After having heard my responses and looking over the transcript, he commented, "There is not much here."

I protested, "I professed Jesus when I was only 12. I love him." I realized I had not done nearly enough and I began sobbing, "I let Him down. I know I let Him down."

St. Peter quietly asked, "Were you not taught that the closer you walk with Jesus the less likely you are to let Him down?"

A long pause ensued. Then St. Peter intoned pleasantly, "Enter, Private Donaldson."

I awoke with a start. The command for Private Donaldson to enter Heaven seemed distant and faint as if in a dream.

Surprisingly, however, St. Peter's words still seem clear enough. "The closer you walk with Jesus, the less likely you are to let Him down."

LAWYER OVERKILL

A news item on my car radio rekindled memories.

The radio news reporter announced that an Eleventh Circuit Court of Appeals hearing that morning (May 11, 2000) concerned Elian Gonzales, the 6-year-old Cuban boy caught in a legal tussle between the United States and Cuba. The child had been taken at gunpoint from his haven in Miami by a federal SWAT team and flown to the Washington area.

A lot of hoopla had surrounded the youngster following his rescue at sea several months earlier after his mother had drowned trying to reach the United States.

The newscaster stated that a group of lawyers, 10 from the Justice Department, had been in the Eleventh Circuit courtroom. The number 10 had caught my attention because of the Department of Justice Civil Rights Division overkill that occurred in Birmingham in the summer of 1981.

Shortly after I was sworn in as U.S. Attorney on June 1 of that year, a lawyer from the Justice Department's Civil Rights Division showed up in my office about 9 a.m. He said he had flown from Washington, D.C. to Birmingham the previous evening and that he had a hearing in district court at 10 a.m.

At the hearing the judge asked him if he was present for the matter at hand, to which the lawyer replied, "Yes, Your Honor." Those were his only words — no papers were filed, no argument made. Nothing was required of government counsel. The case was passed to a later date.

Back in my office I asked, "What are your plans?"

"Flying to D.C. at 2 p.m.," he answered.

The following week another DOJ attorney flew to Birmingham and dropped by my office. I asked why he was here. "A case we are interested in is set for 11 this morning; I thought I ought to be present," he replied.

I went to the courtroom to see what was taking place, as I had the week before when the Justice lawyer had spoken only three words.

On this occasion the judge never once addressed the DOJ lawyer, never recognized his presence, nor did the lawyer speak to the judge. His total time in the courtroom was about 30 seconds. The visiting lawyer then walked downstairs to my office.

"What are your plans?" I asked.

"Flying back to D.C. at 2 p.m.," he replied.

Sometime later at the U.S. attorneys' annual conference Attorney General William French Smith opened the floor for any U.S. attorney who chose to speak. I chose to do so, telling the attorney general — in the presence of the assistant attorney general in charge of the Civil Rights Division, William Bradford Reynolds, a few other DOJ personnel and the other 92 U.S. attorneys present — about the visits by the two Civil Rights Division lawyers to Birmingham for no good reason. My point was that I could have tended to each matter with minimum expense to the Department of Justice. I emphasized the visit of the civil rights lawyer who attended a "hearing" without uttering a word.

"General Smith," I explained, "you may be assured that I can say nothing as well as any lawyer."

The U.S. attorneys howled. They did not know me well at the time, but I believe they guessed I had veracity.

So, in the year 2000 there were 10 Department of Justice attorneys at a hearing involving a 6-year-old boy. That's current-day overkill. In 1981 it occurred in a Republican administration; in the Gonzales matter, in a Democrat administration.

Not much has changed, unless perhaps there was a bit more waste when 10 lawyers were involved.

Poor taxpayers.

PUBLIC SCHOOL PRAYER, THEN AND NOW

My wife Patti taught the fifth grade for four years (1961-65) in the Helena Elementary School.

On November 22, 1963, Mr. S.I. Bice, the principal, came to Patti's classroom and told her that he had just heard on the radio that President John F. Kennedy had been shot, but he did not yet know about the president's condition. He then left the room.

Patti told me that she turned to her class and announced, "Children, the president has been shot. We must pray for him." Then it dawned on her that in June of that year the U.S. Supreme Court had outlawed verbal prayer in the public schools of America, thus it would be "illegal" for her to pray. Nonetheless, she paused only momentarily before leading her class in prayer for the president.

A short time later Mr. Bice returned to her room and said that President Kennedy had died soon after the shooting.

Today would her prayer, offered before pupils in a public classroom, be permissible? More specifically, would such a prayer, offered in a DeKalb County (Alabama) schoolroom on behalf of a dying president, violate Federal Judge Ira DeMent's court order enjoining prayer and Bible reading in DeKalb schools?

Sorry, it would.

THE LEGACY

On one of my early morning walks this intriguing thought buzzed in: Can a common man of today leave a worthwhile legacy?

For years after becoming a law professor emeritus, I have included in my exercise program a brisk 40-45 minute walk. Varied thoughts come and go during the walk, and on this occasion I did not explore other questions concerning a legacy — they come later. For now, I put this one on the board:

Is my life worth remembering? By whom might it be remembered?

For how long? If it is remembered for a while, of what significance would that be?

Gracing the walls of the Cumberland Law School are several excellent portraits of school deans in the 19th Century. No person alive today knew any one of them. But they are remembered, at least their names are, as part of Cumberland's history.

Many other people — professors, staff members, students — had a special role in the history of the school, but no portraits identify them. Thus, there is no visible legacy.

Of course, archival records disclose their names, and a little something about each is provided. As a member of the faculty I looked in the files for information on a need to know basis. Very few people see these records or the names.

At yearly Law Day activities Cumberland observes a memorial service for Rascal, a pet mongrel that for years lived on

Cumberland's Lebanon, Tennessee, campus. Is the idea silly? I suppose early 21st Century animal rights activists approve.

Ironically there is no annual memorial service on Cumberland's Birmingham campus for a human being, although the law school has operated more than 150 years. No later than in the 22nd century, when my children and grandchildren will have joined me, I pray, with Jesus in Heaven, no one on earth will remember this father/grandfather. No former law students will remember this law professor, for they, too, will have long ago left their mortal flesh.

They, as I, will have found that life on this planet is short, at best. Does it follow that there is no lasting legacy?

A cemetery monument, a grave marker at Elmwood Cemetery, a picture on a wall — is that all there will be? That surely isn't much, and there is no assurance even those would not be disturbed. They will deteriorate or simply vanish.

My life has been too varied as an Air Force pilot, FBI agent, lawyer, law professor, and with other roles, too rich and filled with joy to believe that when the final semester ends and "school is out" that it's all over.

Suppose that it is, that this life on earth is remembered for only a few years; that whatever legacy there is, is geographically only local and at best very temporary. Does this then answer the question, "Can a common man leave a worthwhile legacy?"

Fortunately, I'm very pleased that 2,000 years ago Jesus answered my question explicitly in His Sermon on the Mount:

"Lay not up for yourselves treasures upon earth…but lay up for yourselves treasures in Heaven." (Matthew 6:19-20)

What a wonderfully gratifying response to my concern. Just think about it: The opportunity to leave a worthwhile legacy is available to every one of us.

MY DOCTORS MAKE HOUSE CALLS

Some say doctors don't make house calls. That statement is belied by my own experience. I've had three of them, the most recent one only a few years ago. Perhaps that is evidence that flukes occur.

I'd like to go back to the first M.D. house call I ever had, the one that saved the life of an 18-year-old college boy.

It was in late August 1940, within two weeks of my 19th birthday and a couple of weeks prior to fall classes at Howard College where I was enrolled for my sophomore year.

I was visiting home in Phenix City. Carlton Shavor and I went to a movie in the evening, talked and ate peanuts afterward. The next morning a pain in my abdomen was so severe I didn't get out of bed.

Mama called Dr. Willis, our family physician, whose office was in Columbus. He soon arrived and poked a finger in my abdomen. When I went through the ceiling, he told Mama, "This lad has appendicitis. We must get him to a hospital immediately." Of course, he meant the hospital where he did surgery.

That day Dr. Willis removed my appendix and I was hospitalized for eight days.

Showing the swollen appendix to me a few days later, the doctor explained that my appendix would have ruptured very soon had it not been removed the day he first saw me.

The appendix was kept in a jar on my hospital room dresser during my stay. What happened to it later I don't know and don't care.

Thinking of that appendectomy and my long hospital stay brought to mind that years later my two sons, Steve and David, had appendectomies when they were in grade school. Each missed classes only five days.

When I remarked to their surgeon that my two boys had had a remarkably fast recovery, he agreed, and referring specifically to their appendectomies, he said, "like taking out a splinter."

The second time a doctor came to my house was in response to my telephoned plea for help.

Waking up one Saturday morning with the worst headache I ever had, an excruciating one, I called Dr. John Ryan, who lived about five blocks from my house in Helena. I asked if he could give comfort to a guy whose head was about to bust. He replied that he would drop by during the morning, which he did.

In geographical terms, Dr. Ryan had an extensive practice. From his residence office in Helena he made house calls over a big chunk of west Shelby County. He attended lots of patients. He told me when he retired that in his 40-year practice he had delivered 4000 babies, usually in the mothers' residence.

During one period of his practice (I don't recall the dates) his fee for a house call delivery was $35. Often he was never paid the fee; on many occasions he accepted a thank you, a few eggs, some home-grown veggies or such.

After looking me over and asking a few questions, he said, "Mumps. You've got the mumps."

In my view, Dr. Ryan was a masterful diagnostician. He had patients with just about every medical ailment that strikes country people. He had developed such an uncanny ability to diagnose correctly (with little equipment) that after his patients came to Birmingham and had thorough, extensive tests, they revealed Dr. Ryan had been right all along.

I'm sure it was a snap for him to diagnose my mumps. The year was 1960. I was a year away from being 40. And he probably read my mind. Yes, mumps usually hits kids, who hardly know it because the effect is so slight. But mumps also hit 40-year-old guys — and the old guys always know!

Where did I catch the mumps? How? That was easy. Son David, 6, had passed them on to me. He obviously didn't know because he didn't slow down at all.

Dr. Ryan advised me to stay away from my law office, to do no lifting, to stay home and lie around. "You don't want the mumps to go down on you," he cautioned.

Notwithstanding Dr. Ryan's house call and his good advice, my headache was severe for seven days. These days if a headache like that one hit me, I would at once think "aneurysm."

Forty-one years later, I had another home visit, this time from my surgeon.

An occurrence at tennis brought on surgery.

In the fall of year 2000 my opponent on the tennis court returned a high bounce with a smashing "kill shot" to my male anatomy.

Damage was done. Not long afterwards, in December, swelling began. On March 8 a urologist drained it, telling me I could make the teaching assignments for the spring term, postponing corrective surgery a couple of months.

In early May 2001, the swelling was substantial and I had a repair performed at Princeton Hospital's one-day surgery center. "One day" is misleading. Although I went to the hospital Thursday morning and came home that afternoon, recovery took more than a day.

The doctor said I would be homebound for two weeks and play no tennis for six weeks. Now I believe him.

Saturday morning after the operation the surgeon arrived at my house at 8:20 a.m. He easily removed the drain from the affected area and said there would be decreasing drainage for several days. That occurred. He also said the opening made for the drain would "self-seal." It did.

After instructing me on further care, he left to see a grandchild play ball at a nearby park.

Some people say doctors no longer make house calls. I realize it has been 70 years since Dr. Willis came to our house and said I had appendicitis, but it's been only 50 years since Dr. Ryan came to the house and said I had mumps.

OK, so what if the three house calls were spread apart many years? A house call is still a house call, isn't it?

JOB OFFERS

Over the years several acquaintances and friends have told me they had had many unsolicited job offers. I've had very few. About all that come to mind are offers from a couple of law firms, three law schools, and a federal agency.

However, I did have two near-misses, two feelers that might have developed had I pursued them.

On Sunday afternoon June 30, 1996, those who had been elected delegates to the Republican Party National Convention (to be held in August in San Diego) met in Montgomery for planning and other discussion.

At the start all of us identified ourselves. I knew many of those present; other names rang a bell, but I had never heard of some.

I sat just behind Governor Fob James. After introductions he turned around and passed me a handwritten note: "Frank, could I see you for a minute before you leave?—Fob".

When our business was finished, the governor said, "I would like to discuss with you the position of Director, Department of Public Safety. Will you call me in the morning?"

I explained to him that my wife and I were leaving home early the next morning, would be traveling on a long-planned trip, and asked if I could call him Tuesday.

He responded, "How long will you be away?"

A couple of weeks I answered.

"Well," he said. "It's not urgent. I'll call you upon your return."

About two and a half years remained on the governor's term, and he wasn't a good bet to be re-elected. He wasn't.

Furthermore, I wasn't sure I needed the headache; the department was short of funds to operate at the level I believed essential. For example, there was a strong need for additional State Troopers. Also, my office as director would have been nearly 100 miles from my Homewood home, and that would have meant lots of time on I-65.

Patti and I discussed some pros and cons, and the cons won. We decided that if the offer were made, it would be declined. Even if I were invited to visit the governor, I would decline.

Two or three weeks after Patti and I returned from the vacation, Governor James called and right off asked what I thought about his naming a veteran DPS officer to be director, calling him by name. That I did not know the man did not deter my prompt response, "Excellent appointment."

Frankly, I felt that an internal promotion would be good for DPS morale; I hope that was the case.

I haven't the faintest notion whether an offer by the governor would have materialized had I shown enthusiasm from his first mention of the subject or had called him during our trip or upon return. I was very satisfied with the way things turned out, pleased that he had broached the matter with me.

At the San Diego convention Patti and I had dinner one evening with Governor and Mrs. James, Mr. and Mrs. Hall Thompson, and Alabama Supreme Court Chief Justice Perry Hooper and Marilyn, his wife. The DPS job was not mentioned.

Should I have been similarly pleased with another "almost, perhaps" offer?

On April 4, 1987, I received a call from Steve Markman, Assistant Attorney General, Office of Legal Policy, U.S. Department of Justice, reminding me of a vacancy (or soon-to-be) on the Eleventh Circuit Court of Appeals. He asked if I might suggest "an attorney of star quality" that I believed would be a good appointment by President Reagan.

I answered promptly, "Yes" and named a local court judge. I added that, in my opinion and that of members of the Alabama bar, the person I had suggested was a fine judge and would serve well on that court.

A few days later I asked the judge I had suggested if he had heard from Attorney General Ed Meese. He said "Yes," then quickly added a comment I won't forget: "I have the best job in the world and am not interested in a change."

A couple of days later Markman (currently a Justice of the Michigan Supreme Court) phoned me again in the U.S. attorney's office. "Need you to give me another name for Attorney General Meese to consider," he said.

"How about the person I suggested earlier?" I asked.

"Not interested."

Thinking of myself as a possible prospect, I inquired, "What age bracket has General Meese set?"

"Forty to sixty," Markman said.

I was 65 and would be 66 by the time the FBI and ABA background checks could be completed and my name placed before the Senate Judiciary Committee.

The thought "Invite me for an interview" entered my mind, but I didn't voice it.

Shortly after Steve's call I mentioned it to my wife. Her response was, "Why didn't you tell him no lawyer in Alabama is more philosophically in tune with President Reagan than you are?"

Steve had made it plain; Meese said age 60 was the max. Patti indicated she thought it unlikely that age 60 was set in concrete. As it turned out, I was no help to Markman and he turned elsewhere for the judge.

To put the foregoing in perspective and to suggest why I received Steve Markman's call in the first instance, it is helpful to go back to some discussions I had had with Attorney General Meese only a few months after he became attorney general in 1985.

I was a member of Meese's advisory committee, made up of 15 U.S. attorneys. At the beginning of each one of our bi-monthly committee meetings, as was my custom (upon the committee's request), I injected a tad of humor. The practice had become an unwritten assignment.

Typically my effort was to bring up something humorous relating to our work in the Department of Justice. On this occasion I mentioned that one of my assistants had recently argued one of my cases before the Eleventh Circuit Court of Appeals. Chief Justice John Godbold presiding over the three-judge panel had told my assistant at the close of his argument, "Counsel, when you return to Birmingham, look United States Attorney Frank Donaldson in the eyes and tell him I said never to come before this court again with an indefensible case."

I paused a moment, then added, addressing Meese and my colleagues, "I represented the appellee." Having lost the case at the trial court level my opponent had appealed. My role on appeal was to uphold the district court judge's decision.

After the advisory committee meeting, I mentioned to Attorney General Meese that I looked forward to the time when

President Reagan "has the opportunity to fill several seats on that particular court."

I'm not sure about other attorneys general, but Ed Meese made it a practice to first solicit well-qualified judicial prospects, then recommend to the president the names of those men and women he believed worthy to sit as judges on the federal circuit courts. He did not take for granted the judicial worthiness of those persons urged by political party officials for appointment to the appeals courts, although he cut them slack for district court judges.

Attorney General Meese made it plain to the U.S. attorneys that no name of a circuit judge would be submitted to the president without Meese's approval.

Meese and I talked with each other on many occasions, even socially. He liked humor and had a bagful of jokes; I, too, had some, so we hit it off real well. He knew where I stood politically, that I was a strong, albeit reasonable, conservative.

Perhaps because of my good relationship with Meese, Patti thinks until this day he would have — for me — lifted his age 60 barrier to a judicial nomination.

Every candidate to be considered for a judgeship was invited to Washington for interviews with several DOJ attorneys. So, had I asked Steve Markman, perhaps I would have been invited to main Justice for interviews. Who knows, I might have become a federal judge.

Big deal. If that had been my burning ambition, a really strong desire to sit on the appellate bench, I certainly would have explored the matter or attempted to do so.

So as things stand, I'll never know whether an offer might have materialized had I suggested myself to be considered as a member of the appeals court.

Be that as it may, I'm not displeased that events developed as they did. President Reagan made a good appointment.

Just as the trial judge said of his position, I have said of mine as a career law professor, "I have the best job in the world and am not interested in a change."

The only curse of academic life is grading exam papers, i.e., judging my students, and that's only twice a year at the end of each semester. Surely there must be more curses for an appellate court judge.

IN REMEMBRANCE

The Pilgrim Congregational Church, "my church" as a boy growing up in Phenix City, Alabama, had a Lord's Supper table located just below the pulpit on the floor of the sanctuary. The table was always there, never moved from its special position, and was also always bare, except when wine and bread, sacraments for use by the congregants during the Communion Celebration, were placed on it.

Deeply embedded in my mind, from the time of my teenage years, perhaps earlier, are the words "This Do In Remembrance of Me," plainly inscribed in large letters on the front of the table. The table was about 5 feet by 3 feet and visible by all worshipers wherever they sat.

The inscribed words could be read from a distance of 7 or 8 pews, even though the communion table was several feet in front of the nearest one.

Today when we have our Communion Celebration in "my church," Dawson Memorial Baptist, in Homewood, Alabama, I see an almost identical table, in size, color, and shape. On the front of it is an inscription of Jesus' charge to his followers, "This Do In Remembrance of Me."

During the special ordinance at Dawson the table is placed on the platform where the pulpit is usually located, some 10 feet from the nearest pew. Nonetheless, the "Remembrance" words are prominently visible to hundreds of worshippers.

Yesterday evening during the Lord's Supper celebration at Dawson my thoughts went back to Pilgrim. As I observed the elements on the table before me and the inscription, "This Do In Remembrance of Me," I joyfully realized that for more than three-score ten years I have worshipped in remembrance.

IT COULD HAPPEN TO YOU

Late one Monday morning I completed my brisk 40-minute walk in the Lakeshore Foundation gym. Because my plans were to go from there to lunch I headed to the restroom to wash my hands. An elderly man and woman were very near the men's room door and I noticed she was assisting him to walk.

I got an immediate feeling that the lady was debating with herself whether to accompany her husband into the men's room or whether to let go of her hold on his arm and hope that he could manage himself. I paused near the door, believing they had a bit of a plight. I asked, "Could I lend a hand?" The woman quickly responded, "Yes, my husband," nodding toward the latrine. I reached out and put my right hand under his left elbow. We slowly moved through the doorway. As we did the lady said, "You will need to pull his trousers down — and his shorts." I nodded.

At the urinal I unbuckled his belt, lowered his zipper, slid his trousers down — and his shorts. When the old gentleman completed his effort I pulled up his shorts and trousers and fastened the belt buckle. When I zipped up the zipper on his pants my fingers got damp. He had had a bit of incontinence.

As we moved toward the wash bowl the old fellow stopped, turned slowly toward me, looked directly into my eyes, and softly said, "Thank you."

After washing his hands, using very little water, he dried them with one small paper towel. Walking toward the exit door, I said to him, "Seems to me you grew up during the Depression."

He didn't noticeably respond.

When we stepped outside the latrine into the hallway his wife was standing near the door, close to where we had left her. I said, "I'm sure your husband was caught up in the Depression — he used only one small paper towel to dry his hands."

She responded, "Yes, we were both there." Then she added, "Yesterday I was washing my hands in our bathroom sink when my little grandson said, 'Grandmother, you don't have much water.' He had noticed I had turned the faucet on, but had a small stream. I told him 'I don't use much water. I have to pay the water bill.'"

She and I then talked a little while and learned we had three mutual friends. Her husband appeared to listen, seemed to silently join in the conversation, but said nothing.

Ready to leave, I said, "I hope to see you two soon in the gym." At that juncture the lady walked near me, to one side, gently rubbed the palm of one hand over my back, again and again in a circular motion. I'm sure I gave her a puzzled expression. She quickly picked up on it, "Just feeling for your wings," she said with a sweet smile.

I was taken aback. "No, no, not me." I may have remonstrated too assertively.

I immediately walked into the men's room, straight to the sink, where I washed my hands real good with soap and water. The thought then struck me, "An angel wouldn't need to do this."

I dried my hands with two paper towels, promptly left the building and met my wife for lunch.

A FAREWELL SALUTE

To emulate the best and become a top-quality professor isn't easy. Did I make it? Only my students can answer.

THREE TOP TEACHERS

The question was: "Who was your most outstanding teacher, aside from parents?"

Three stand out: A flight instructor, a faculty member at the FBI Academy and a law professor. None of my public school teachers are included, although several I remember with fondness.

As for college, I recall several professors with much favor. Because I didn't always study diligently, I didn't appreciate them as I should have. Other things took precedence.

The Flight Instructor

After I entered the Army Air Forces in 1942 and became an aviation cadet, nothing was more important to me than learning to fly military aircraft.

I was particularly fortunate to have been assigned to Lieutenant Robert Froman as my flight instructor. He is the first of my three "standouts."

We were at Randolph Field, Texas. My first flight with Lt. Froman was September 8, 1942, on my 21st birthday.

From the very beginning we hit it off. I liked him and I think he liked me. Not only did Lt. Froman demonstrate excellent pilot skills, his teaching technique caused me to look forward to each flight. My self-confidence grew — perhaps soared. He consistently got my best effort. I'm sure he must have brought out the best in his other three students. Sometimes I wondered: Does this officer have a degree in psychology?

At the outset Lt. Froman made clear that his primary goal was for his students to become the best pilots in the cadet class.

A particularly discomfiting experience illustrates the lieutenant's skill with a trainee pilot. We were practicing spins in a BT-13. My military airtime until I was commissioned was mostly in that type aircraft.

The lieutenant had dual objectives: to teach me how to do a controlled spin and what to do if the plane went into an inadvertent spin. During my first spin exercise my feet slipped because my seat belt was too loose; one foot went under a pedal and I had trouble freeing it, so that we spun and spun and spun. Finally I freed the foot, pulled the plane out and leveled off.

The lieutenant said calmly, "Better tighten your belt." I wasn't sure what he might say next, but after a pause all he added was, "Good recovery." After we landed, he seemed amused by the whole thing.

Once just before or just after a flight, I asked Lieutenant Froman how he liked being "stuck" in the training command as a flight instructor. His response was almost classic, "I would like to go overseas but there's only one me. As an instructor I'll train four of you to go into combat in my place."

Presumably his trainees would ultimately go into combat. But it didn't turn out that way for all his cadets. For one, I got "stuck" in the training command as a flight instructor.

My own Army Air Forces instructor days began shortly after I was commissioned in December 1942. I racked up hundreds of hours teaching cadets to fly.

Although every one of my students performed his flight tests satisfactorily after the training period, I never was able to duplicate the one-on-one instruction skills of Lt. Froman.

Not long before our cadet Class of 42-X was graduated, the lieutenant was transferred to Army Air Forces Headquarters. Thus I lost a great instructor, but the Pentagon got a top-quality officer, one of my "three most outstanding teachers. I wished that in later years I could have seen him and told him so.

The Law Professor

After class one day a student mentioned to me that she had been attending class for 18 of her 24 years and that she had never been as upset as she was with me. She added, "You embarrassed me. No," she bore down, "I was humiliated."

I apologized, making clear that what I had said to her in class was not intended to cause her psychic injury. However, I tried to explain that in the legal profession "it's to be expected that feelings worn on a sleeve will be knocked off."

I later asked myself if the best law teacher I ever had would have caused the same student to complain to him as she had complained to me. My answer: most likely not.

If M. Leigh Harrison had embarrassed that young woman in class, she probably would have blushed and appeared flustered, as many students did, but she would have understood that his incessant questions were drilled to all students, individually and collectively. They were meant to make us ready for legal combat.

Harrison, for several years dean of the UA Law School (including my student years there in 1952-54), was a renowned and highly respected Alabama scholar, and a person who had no detectable foolishness in his being.

I have pondered why I consider Dean Harrison one of my three greatest teachers. The answer is motivation. He made me study, and to think; that is, he caused me to want to study and think. I also shuddered at the thought of going to his class unprepared.

I had the course in Contracts from Dean Harrison in my first semester at Alabama. The tone was set and an A resulted.

Several years later Dean Arthur Weeks of the Cumberland Law School told me that he needed a Contracts professor and asked if I was interested. I indicated yes, whereupon he asked, "What grades did you make in Contracts?" I told him an A each semester and my response settled the matter. Dean Weeks also had been a law student under Dean Harrison. And Weeks knew that Harrison was not known in Farrah Hall for giving generous As.

I enjoyed teaching Contracts (1963-72) in both day and evening classes (the latter, 1965-72), no doubt in part because I was able to use my extensive notes from Dean Harrison's classes.

When I left teaching Contracts and shifted to Civil Procedure courses as my primary field in 1973, I gave my notes to Brad Bishop, who assumed the role of Contracts professor at Cumberland.

Brad had been one of my students in Contracts (A both semesters), so I thought it also appropriate to give him my notes from Dean Harrison's classes. Brad was selected by students several times as Cumberland's "Professor of the Year."

I like to think that there may be a connection with Brad's success as Contracts teacher and his use of my notes from the Contracts classes of the late great Dean Leigh Harrison.

The FBI Agent

Dallas Mobley, Georgia native assigned in 1947 to the FBI Academy at Quantico, Virginia, was known to all of us agents-to-be in school at the academy as a former high school teacher. He had told us that he became an agent because "those senior high school girls got to looking too good," and as he put it, "another calling was imperative lest there be trouble."

So, an FBI agent is the third of my greatest teachers.

During the nearly three-month course, Mobley's work hours were 9 a.m. to 6 p.m. with an hour off for lunch, less several off-days and partial days while we new guys were involved in a variety of training projects under other instructors.

Mobley handled a tough job masterfully. Not that the job was tough because we were difficult students; to the contrary, we were anxious to absorb all learning possible. But the scope of Mobley's material was unusually extensive.

FBI jurisdiction covered about 300 federal statutes. Part of Mobley's job was to teach us the elements in many of those statutes so that we could understand what was necessary for a prosecutor to prove to obtain a conviction. That meant we were to make sure our investigation was thorough, that we left no opening for a subject to slip through in the cases we presented to the U.S. attorney for indictment and prosecution.

Our academy instructors also dealt with a myriad of internal operating procedures of the bureau, dozens of rules and requirements, including ethical issues and general agent behavior. On the latter Mobley was very descriptive. For example, he mentioned an agent working in New York City who became infatuated with a Broadway showgirl. The agent met her in the evening after her show, stayed up late, and overslept in the morning. The quality of the agent's work deteriorated and he was fired.

As always, Mobley spiced the account with humor. He commented on the dismissed agent, "Who knows, maybe he would do it again!"

A similar "horror" story recalled an agent who met a beautiful girl while traveling by train from Denver to Memphis, his new assignment. Night came on as the train crossed Kansas. In the early evening the young woman invited the agent to her adjoining sleeper car. Attired in pajamas he left his car and spent the night in her berth. During the night the train pulled into Kansas City and switched some cars to Chicago, some to Memphis.

When the agent awoke next morning, he learned that his clothes, badge, gun, credentials, etc., were en route to Memphis, his intended destination. But he was bound for Chicago.

"Besides the humiliation," Mobley recounted, "the now-unemployed officer had to pay his own way home." Then typical of Mobley, he commented, "Who knows, perhaps the evening was worth the firing."

The two anecdotes suggest: (1) Dallas Mobley seldom lectured without humor, and (2) his lectures included illustrations and stories that were pertinent, relevant, beneficial, and easy for us to remember.

Dean M. Leigh Harrison of the UA Law School, my law professor extraordinaire, used many hypotheticals to help his students to think-think, but he certainly was not humorous. His comments always were serious as were his facial expressions.

What a contrast between the law professor and the FBI instructor. Yet, no one of us ever thought of the latter, with his pervasive humor, as not being serious despite the laughter he provoked.

From time to time in my teaching I have mimicked each of my great teachers. The result is a kind of mix. But it ain't easy!

LETTING GO

One magnificently beautiful morning in late October I walked from the Cumberland Law School building to the Samford University food court to get coffee and a Chick-Fil-A sandwich for breakfast. This trip I made fairly regularly on Tuesday and Thursday mornings just prior to teaching my 7:35 a.m. law class.

As I crossed the campus area between the university library and the food court building, I looked south across the campus, observed a number of autumn's multi-colored leaves falling on manicured grass, noticed a mockingbird in a nearby bush and saw beds of petunias still in bloom.

A fleeting thought that first crossed my mind immediately grabbed complete hold of me as I watched the colorful oak leaves floating downward. Like the falling leaves, I thought, I too, soon will be turning loose and letting go. The leaves had had a short spring and summer, as I have had a short nearly two-score years as a law professor on this campus. My days here are numbered. In a short time I shall leave this splendid place. Then I asked myself, should I thank God for giving me these wonderful years, or should I simply cry because they are about to end?

During the next few days I posed the question to a few of my relatives and friends. Some responded, "Thank God, of course." Others replied, "Cry. It's no sin for a grown man to shed tears when he grieves." Still others said, "What's the problem with tearful thankfulness?"

Another year has passed. Again I've just walked over to the food court for coffee and a bite of breakfast before class. The morning is magnificent; the campus is beautiful. Once again the colorful leaves are turning loose and floating down. I don't know yet when I will let go, turn the last page in a law book and no longer walk across the campus in early morning or at all. But this is certain: I am today a year deeper into my autumn. And when the end time comes, I'm sure to have moist eyes. These years of professional joy have sped by. Spring was here only yesterday.

Epilogue: More than 5 years have passed since the last paragraph was written. And it is really springtime: Today I walked to the food court before class — the last time.

For many semesters I've kicked off Cumberland's earliest morning class session at 7:35, alternately teaching Pretrial Practice and Equitable Remedies.

This morning, scanning the campus grounds, I saw bountiful green leaves above and fresh multi-colored flowers below; spring in its glory. Alas, autumn for the professor. I don't like letting go, especially having yet a sharp mind, strong body and willing spirit; but, an ever-worsening hearing impairment dooms the teaching career.

Hearing aids have not kept up with the hearing loss. Even so, I could do another semester or so if my students were all male, but about 40 percent of them each semester are women whose soft voices pass me by. As happy as I am to see the influx of female law students they have nonetheless sped up my departure.

So, today the bell has rung for my last class, and in May when exam papers have been graded, my 43 years of law teaching at Cumberland will end. Thank God for giving me the golden opportunity to be a classroom professor to 4,500 different students enrolled in the Cumberland School of Law (1962-2005). I am at this moment filled with gratitude.

On April 25, 2005 the words of Jesus Christ are on my mind:

"I am come that they might have life,

and that they might have it more abundantly."

John 10:10b KJV

Law Professor - 2005
43 years at Cumberland School of Law
Samford University

Donaldson Family — Christmas 2008
Dawson Memorial Baptist Church

No man is more blessed than I. Having lived upon the beautiful Planet Earth for four-fifths of the 20th Century (minus one year) and a decade of the 21st in the greatest nation upon that planet, I am a beneficiary of the Lord's promise of abundant life. I give thanks to Almighty God, and do so with a heart filled with gratitude.

I hope the stories in this book speak to the truth of this testimony.

February 28, 2011

Made in the USA
Lexington, KY
21 October 2011